The Better Friend

"In an individualized and lonely world, Valentine encourages readers through her book, *The Better Friend,* showing us that we are made for community. She addresses the lies that hold us back from deep connection and speaks the truth on how we can begin to find better friends in order to become all God made us to be."

—MADISON PREWETT TROUTT, bestselling author of *The Love Everybody Wants,* podcast host of *Stay True,* and speaker

"If you've ever felt overlooked or rejected, or you've questioned whether pursuing friendships is even worth it, this book is for you. In *The Better Friend,* Valentine speaks with honesty and vulnerability about the challenges we face in our relationships with friends. She beautifully expresses the thoughts we've all had but haven't said out loud, guiding us to reflect on where we may need to grow or let go. Through practical insights, tips, and 'the better friend challenge,' Valentine teaches us how to nurture the meaningful, healthy friendships we all long for and deserve. This is the book you need if you're ready to find—and become—a better friend."

—ASHLEY MORGAN JACKSON, bestselling author of *Tired of Trying,* speaker, and writer for Proverbs 31 Ministries

"One of the most important things in a young girl's life is to know how to find a good friend and how to be a good friend.

Our friendships shape who we become and how we see the world and teach us how to love those around us. This is why I am so thankful that Grace Valentine has written this incredibly relatable, realistic guide on how to be a better friend and how to choose better friends. Filled with twelve truths about how to find, keep, and maintain healthy friendships, this book is honest, raw, and real. The encouragement and truth found in these pages feels like sitting across the table from a wise older sister who has your best interests at heart and is always ready to give you the best advice in every situation you might face. I believe this book is a must-read for every young woman."

—MELANIE SHANKLE, *New York Times* bestselling author
of *Nobody's Cuter Than You* and *Here Be Dragons*

"Valentine's heart as a good friend who champions others is evident in everything she does, and I can't wait to see how this book will inspire and encourage you. I believe her words will lead you to deeper connections in your friendships and in your relationship with Jesus."

—LANEY RENE, founder of The One He Loves

"Many women and girls channel energy into *finding* the right friends—but very few channel that same energy into *being* the right friend. This book reverses that dynamic, and I'm so thankful for Valentine's ability to relate to the pain of friendship struggles while also calling us up to a better way. This message is for all ages, and anyone who takes it to heart will see their relationships transformed!"

—KARI KAMPAKIS, bestselling author of *Love Her Well*
and host of the *Girl Mom* podcast

"*The Better Friend* is an encouraging, inspiring, and reflective book. Just like the author's heart, her book is a true reflection of what the Holy Spirit can do through experiences in friendships to reflect the love of Christ. Valentine states, 'Good friendships are waiting for you, but you'll never meet them if you're too busy begging for a table that was never meant for you in the first place.' She equips us to pick up our chairs and walk toward God's table—the one He's made for us."

—REECE WEAVER ALLMAN

The Better Friend

the
Better
Friend

**12 Truths to Shift from Shallow and
One-Sided Connections to Vibrant
Friendships**

Grace
Valentine

WaterBrook

Details in some anecdotes and stories have been changed to protect
the identities of the persons involved.

A WaterBrook Trade Paperback Original

Library of Congress Cataloging-in-Publication Data
Names: Valentine, Grace, author.
Title: The better friend : 12 truths to shift from shallow and one-sided
connections to vibrant friendships / Grace Valentine.
Description: Colorado Springs : WaterBrook, [2025] | "A WaterBrook trade
paperback original." | Includes bibliographical references.
Identifiers: LCCN 2024034758 | ISBN 9780593601372 (trade paperback ;
acid-free paper) | ISBN 9780593601389 (ebook)
Subjects: LCSH: Friendship—Religious aspects. | Female friendship.
Classification: LCC BV4647.F7 V34 2025 |
DDC 241/.6762082—dc23/eng/20241125
LC record available at https://lccn.loc.gov/2024034758

Printed in the United States of America on acid-free paper

waterbrookmultnomah.com
penguinrandomhouse.com

2 4 6 8 9 7 5 3 1

For details on special quantity discounts for bulk purchases, contact
specialmarketscms@penguinrandomhouse.com.

The authorized representative in the EU for product safety and compliance
is Penguin Random House Ireland, Morrison Chambers, 32 Nassau Street,
Dublin D02 YH68, Ireland, https://eu-contact.penguin.ie.

To my best friends, my future bridesmaids, my future dance floor friends, and the people who have shown up for me over and over again. Whether we met in childhood, in class, at summer camp, as girls learning lessons the hard way and listening to "Closer" by The Chainsmokers a little too much, or in our twenties, thank you. Thanks for being good friends and making me better.

And for the lonely girl holding this book, this is also for you. I have been you, and I am praying that as you read these words, you will find peace from Jesus, unreasonable love, confidence to not give up, and friendships that make you better. Better is coming when you do life with the Giver of life.

contents

introduction: "i'm always the better friend." ix

truth 1: know the difference between miserable
comforters and unreasonable love 3

truth 2: community is created, not found 11
7 reminders about finding and keeping friends of goodness   22

truth 3: give grace, not excuses 28
7 truths for loving radically but trusting wisely   35

truth 4: comparison kills community 40
7 reminders about comparison   46

truth 5: don't beg to sit at tables Jesus hasn't prepared
for you 51
7 ways to cultivate deep community without being exclusive   57

truth 6: call your friends up, not out 64
7 reminders about calling friends up, not out   68

truth 7: know the difference between loyal to a fault and
loyal to your calling 75

7 truths about loyalty   82

truth 8: beware of your mess, and show grace 86

7 questions to ask your friends regularly   96

truth 9: friendship breakups are hard but can still
be holy 98

7 signs it's time to end a friendship   107

truth 10: sometimes we're the bad friend 113

7 ways to handle reconciliation   117

truth 11: receive the blessing of friendship. 122

7 reminders about accepting love better   126

truth 12: leave people better 133

7 truths about healthy friendships   138

bonus: 7 reminders about avoiding gossip 141

"i'm always the better friend."

I've made a lot of important decisions in my life. After my freshman year of college, I decided to stop using six layers of eyeliner. I've already determined that when low-rise jeans come back into style, I will never participate in that horrendous trend again. I made the decision to leave my home state for college. And I chose to run a half-marathon with little to no training. (I survived but couldn't walk for three business days.) But honestly, nothing was as important as deciding both to walk with Jesus and to walk with better friends.

I truly believe that's true for each of us. The most important decisions you will ever make are about whom you will walk with in this wild adventure of life.

I get that it sounds cheesy. But I know it's true because I have been in friendships that were shallow, one-sided, or hurtful or that just made me feel invisible. Sometimes it was their fault, and sometimes it was just because we truly weren't better together. Maybe you resonate with the feeling of being overlooked, betrayed, or let down by the friendships in your life. Maybe you're tired of superficial relationships and long for rich, life-giving connections. When friendships aren't vibrant and fulfilling, chances are, we overthink, overcompensate, and feel overwhelmed.

We tend to overthink our daily lives when no one is growing alongside us or going deep with us. This might look like having friends who shrug their shoulders if we get drunk, who lead us to gossip instead of encourage, who simply don't care whether we're being our best selves, or who stir up fear with the things they're telling others about us.

When we surround ourselves with shallow or fake friendships, we overcompensate by searching for our worth in beauty, work, school, popularity, and things that just don't matter. Instead of working hard to become our best selves, we waste precious time obsessing over being who we're not. Instead of being loving, we try to prove we are worth loving.

These kinds of friendships make us feel insecure and, worse, lead us away from God's best, causing us to miss out on the experience of God's love and a sense of belonging. When we don't feel that we belong or that we are seen and loved, we become overwhelmed by this chaotic world. Daily tasks cause consistent stress and anxiety because we don't find the joy of Christ in sharing mundane moments with a loving community. If the people around us only make us feel alone, we become overwhelmed by the thought—and probable truth—that maybe they don't really care about us. When we have to consistently fight to feel seen by others, we often fail to see the God who sees us.

Shallow friendships really suck, right? In a culture obsessed with popularity, social climbing, and what others can give you, it's easy to get stuck in these relationships. But I like to think you picked up this book because, like me, you are over one-sided, fake friendships. Proverbs 17:17 says, "A friend loves at all times, and a brother is born for a time of adversity." A true friend loves you all the time and is such a gift in this crazy world. But so often we settle for

- friends who include us *sometimes,*
- friends who are fun *sometimes,* or
- friends who listen to us *sometimes.*

We prioritize fun, success, and the feeling of being wanted over friends who make us better people. We can't expect friendships that are perfect, and we have to remember we can't literally be invited everywhere, but I like to think it is holy to want friends who seek to love us at all times. And I don't think you and I are selfish for desiring this. In fact, this is a holy desire.

Maybe God has shown you recently that you have *sometimes* friends. This doesn't mean you need to cut them off completely and shame them. But it does mean that maybe we should all learn how to love radically and trust wisely.

And that is why I wrote this book: because I have been in your shoes and at one point felt the desire for people who were *all-time* friends and sisters I could lean on. And when we cultivate, identify, and cherish these God-given friendships— instead of always overthinking, overcompensating, and feeling overwhelmed—we feel the presence of God, who is over it all.

When we find better friends, we become better people and grow to know God better.

When we find better friends, we become better people and grow to know God better. And when we become good friends who care well for those around us, we experience not only the joy that comes from being a blessing but also Christ in us being a light to those He led us to.

Since this whole book is on friendship, I feel like it would be wrong if I didn't introduce myself. So, hi. I'm Grace Valentine. In my almost three decades of life, I've learned a lot about friendship disappointments, friendship breakups, and one-sided friendships. I've experienced the heartache of loneliness as well as the joy of vibrant and life-giving friendships.

I've cried over boys I dated, boys I didn't date, period cramps, being laid off and struggling to pay bills, losing someone too soon, a bad hangover, the movie *The Holiday*, and having "nothing to wear"—and over friendships.

Meeting a new friend calls for some small talk to show you're a trustworthy and somewhat-interesting human. So, to that effect, I love sushi, I have an older brother who keeps me humble, I am from south Louisiana, and I did not study abroad in Italy like it seems every other twentysomething did. I also didn't go to New York City at Christmastime this year like everyone else. I talk too fast and too loud and sometimes get misunderstood. I have moved multiple times in my life but most recently to Atlanta, Georgia. Turned out, I could fit everything I own in my old Honda Civic and just drive off to a whole new state. I found myself back at square one—living in an apartment by myself for the first time and learning how to survive winter after moving from the Sunshine State. But even harder was learning how to make friends again while keeping my long-distance friendships, avoid comparing myself to those around me, date boys from both online and the wild (aka real life), and become my best self.

Truthfully, for the longest time, what hindered me from becoming a better friend and finding better friendships was how pathetic I felt. This sounds dumb to admit, but if we are going to talk about shallow, one-sided, and disappointing friendships, I have to be honest about my own shallowness. I was embarrassed and frustrated because I always felt like the better friend. Too often it felt like me trying a whole lot and my friends forgetting about me or just not wanting to be in good friendships. There was a time it really irritated me, and like so many of our frustrations these days, it all started with *a social media post*.

The post that caused me to spiral was simply a birthday message. Five girls who had all met each other because of me took a picture together by a pool at a fancy hotel, drinking margaritas and eating truffle french fries. The caption read, "Happy birthday to our girl Annabelle! To know you is to love you! Today was the best day celebrating you."

So it's Annabelle's (not her real name) *birthday weekend, and everyone I know was invited but me?*

"To know you is to love you" . . . *blah.* My thoughts continued to spin as my insecurity grew. They knew her only because of me, so why couldn't they actually treat me like a friend? They liked my friend recommendations but not me?

Maybe to know Grace Valentine is to not love her enough to invite her.

So there I was, staring at my cheap popcorn ceiling, crying alone on a Saturday afternoon with no fancy french fries and no luxury pool, feeling resentful and pathetic. I introduced them and helped them find their best friends, then got kicked to the curb and forgotten. *If they are having these birthday weekend trips together, then I know they also have a group text without me. I bet they even have a cute group text name with an inside joke and they update each other on every detail of their lives.*

Obviously, I wasn't just upset about this one post. I was upset because I thought that by my early twenties, I would have figured out this whole friendship thing. Maybe the post bothered me so much because I had watched so many sitcoms where a cute friend group had nine seasons of adventures but I had only a random assortment of "almost friends" who probably didn't even know I had a brother. The post reminded me that I was lonely, felt discontent, and had shallow friendships.

Now I can look back and see that I couldn't control how that friend group viewed me or whether they invited me, but I could control how I reacted. And my reaction made things worse. It wasn't healthy, holy, or good. That Saturday afternoon when I scrolled and saw that picture, I reacted out of my insecurity. I felt pathetic because I allowed disappointment to write lies about my worth. To be really honest about my emotions, I would say I wasn't just struggling with friendships—I was struggling with being content in my singleness, finances, and more. And I was doubting God's goodness.

I know I'm not the only one who has felt overwhelmed by friendships. Maybe you, too, have come across pictures of your "friends" hanging out without you and spiraled just like I did. Spiraling is the common reaction when we feel insecure about our friendships. It also looks like the freak-out we do when we wonder if a current friend is ghosting us. And it's that feeling we get when we reflect on a friend breakup from five years ago and realize we cared more than she ever did. Spiraling can happen when we feel lonely or when we meet new friends and feel insecure.

Friendship can be hard. It sometimes requires a lot of emotional labor. And while trying to create community, we may find ourselves fighting through trust issues from past hurts and overthinking new connections. Finding community can be a challenge because—let's face it—you don't just stumble upon a group of girlfriends who also love queso and make you feel happy, joyful, and seen. Community doesn't happen overnight; it usually starts with an awkward hello and the hope that a current stranger will become a lifelong companion. Friendship requires vulnerability, but when done right, it leads us to our best and God's best. And when we find better people and seek to be better ourselves, holy friendships become comforting, clear, and Christlike.

So let this book be your reminder that it is good to desire a community that cares for you and others well. You're not pathetic for caring—in fact, it is great that you do.

It is good to desire a community that cares for you and others well.

This book will give you twelve truths to help you find, identify, and keep vibrant friendships. You'll also learn how to react when your friends inevitably disappoint you, leave you, or confuse you. But there is one simple truth I want you to know as we start this journey: Friendship is worth it.

When I look back over my life, I see the pain from friendships but also the incredible joy.

In middle school, I was teased by some peers, and a girl named Paige stood up for me and defended me. I got to stand by her side as a bridesmaid in her wedding over a decade later.

In early high school, a group of girls who were my "friends" often left me out and talked about me. This brought me closer to my friend Chloe. Today, she is my favorite person to FaceTime.

One day in college, while struggling to find my group, I was eating alone outside my dorm. A girl who was walking by asked if I wanted to hang out. She has become my best friend. I am thankful that eating alone one time at age eighteen led me to many dinners, lunches, and much laughter with Britta.

When I was a young adult mourning the end of a best guy friendship because of feelings, confusion, and boundaries, my friend Nora (who knew us both) stood by my side, sent me comforting handwritten notes, and reminded me of my worth. She didn't make me feel crazy for crying over a guy I never dated. She cared for me well.

In my twenties, when singleness made me feel lonely and all my good friends were getting married, having babies, and (I thought) forgetting about me, I met two roommates who became close friends. We cooked salmon, did ice-cream runs, and watched all the seasons of *Scandal* together. My singleness and loneliness led me to Ramsey and Maile.

When I moved to Atlanta and knew maybe two people by name, my friend Mckenzie introduced me to all her friends. What started off as a scary season ended up becoming a blessing because of her inviting spirit.

So, yes, friendship is hard, but our lonely times often lead to moments of real connection. Our hardest goodbyes lead to beautiful, unexpected blessings. And maybe if you're feeling lonely, bitter, or stuck in one-sided friendships, you just need to start this journey by remembering that God is leading you to a miracle. James 1:12 says, "Blessed is the man who remains steadfast under trial, for when he has stood the test he will receive the crown of life, which God has promised to those who love him" (ESV).

In our current culture where everyone is online, sarcasm can quickly become mean, and confusion is common, friendship is often under trial. When you stand steadfast and trust the Lord during the loneliness, disappointment, and insecurity, you receive something better than life going "your way"—you receive His presence. And when you receive God's presence, He will lead you to a community that cares because He cares for you and loves you.

Don't doubt yourself if you gave friendship your all while others didn't. Instead, celebrate that you cared, because that's Christ in you. Caring is a good thing. Stand firm in His love, in living a loving life, and trust that God has promised you His goodness.

the better friend challenge

Take a few minutes to reflect on your current friendships.

- When was the last time you overthought, felt the need to overcompensate, or felt overwhelmed because of friendships? Why did you feel this way?

- What does it mean to celebrate Christ in you when you care more than others seem to? How can you be thankful for the times you loved big?

- What would it mean for you to find friends who love you well?

Write a prayer asking God to reveal His truth to you about your current and future friendships. Ask Him to not only teach you contentment in your present circumstances but also give you boldness and hope to create better community.

The Better Friend

truth 1

know the difference between miserable comforters and unreasonable love

I wasn't cool in middle school. While all the cool kids got picked up in carpools, I spent thirty-five minutes riding down random streets in a sweaty school bus waiting for my bus stop. I wore glasses that I got at the same store where you can buy mayonnaise, toothpaste, and tires, so they weren't glamorous. I didn't even have braces yet because I didn't finish losing my baby teeth until age fifteen. You probably have a young cousin or niece who finished losing them at seven years old, but I was a late bloomer. And late bloomers are hardly ever cool. My front teeth each leaned in opposite directions, and there was a big gap in between them. I didn't make the middle school cheer team, and I struggled to fit in with the girls whom I desperately wanted to call my friends.

I wanted so badly to sit at the cool-girl lunch table. All those girls had Vera Bradley lunch boxes while I had the "interesting"-looking school lunch every day. Even the teachers favored the popular group. The cool girls could do toe touches and, even in middle school, knew how to talk to boys. But no matter how hard I tried, I wasn't included. I remember sitting near them and listening in on their conversations about sleepovers and their Webkinz collections.

One day, I approached one of the girls and asked what Vera Bradley pattern her lunch box was. When she said, "Cherry blossom, *duh!*" everyone laughed and turned away from me.

Exclusion stings.

Now that I'm older, I wear contacts, have straighter teeth after finally getting braces (even though I should've worn my retainer more), and even occasionally get a lot of likes on Instagram. But despite all that, I've noticed that I still feel like that awkward middle schooler approaching the cool-girl table of friendship.

See, no amount of followers, dinner parties, happy hours, sorority date parties, or invites can make up for the bullying, hurts, isolation, and empty lunch tables you experienced growing up. In fact, you need to find contentment in who God made you to be before you can truly find friends who love you in a way that reflects His love.

No amount of followers, dinner parties, happy hours, sorority date parties, or invites can make up for the bullying, hurts, isolation, and empty lunch tables you experienced growing up.

When I noticed I had mainly shallow and one-sided friendships, my first reaction was to blame everyone else: *Why couldn't* they *be better friends? Why couldn't* they *choose me, care for me, and show up for me?* I blamed my disappointment on their inability to see my worth. Although sometimes I truly was betrayed or let down by others, I can now see that the disappointment actually started with *my* inability to see my worth.

In *The Perks of Being a Wallflower*, a novel by Stephen Chbosky, there is a popular quote that many of us have heard and lived out: "We accept the love we think we deserve."[1] I've spent too long feeling insecure and inadequate and therefore settling for superficial friendships. I couldn't change how those people treated me or saw me, but I could change how I saw myself and what I accepted. When I walked confidently, understanding my worth, I found people who celebrated and cared for me.

So what I want to ask you, new friend to new friend, is this: How have past friendships, hurts, betrayals, exclusion, bullying, and insecurity shaped the way you view yourself? Do you believe this has affected the way you search for friendships?

When I think about middle school Grace who wanted so badly to sit with the cool girls, I can't help but also be reminded of the early-twentysomething Grace who moved to a new city and once again wanted so badly to be in the cool girls' group text, be invited to their fancy brunches, and somehow have such cool friendships. But like I said, no amount of table invites, friends, followers, or likes can make up for the insecurity and empty lunch tables you had in childhood.

Friends can comfort you and cheer you on, but it is up to you to accept yourself.

Once you commit to following God along the path to better friends, He will often start the journey in your own heart. And He'll help you discover three things:

Better confidence in who He made you to be. You don't need perfect confidence. You will still face bad days, insecurity, and exclusion. But you must learn to accept your quirks and be okay if others don't see your worth. Don't let someone else's inability to see your value stop you from walking in confidence. Make sure your security comes from God, not from others accepting you, adding you to the group text, or inviting you to their lunch tables. Friends can comfort you and cheer you on, but it is up to you to accept yourself.

Better contentment when life isn't going how you wish. You can find contentment in lonely seasons when you remember the friend you already have in Jesus. Jesus is your Savior, your Lord, and also your friend. John 15:15 says, "I no longer call you servants, because a servant does not know his master's business. Instead, I have called you friends, for everything that I learned from my Father I have made known to you." Jesus spoke this to His disciples, the men who followed Him on this earth and documented His miracles, but I believe He was also thinking of you and me when He said this. Jesus made His life, character, sorrows, and strength known to you. So you, too, should let Jesus in, share your life with Him, and call Him your friend. Once you seek Jesus as your friend, you have a friend for life who creates miracles unexpectedly.

Better discernment when it comes to friendships. Interestingly, when I was almost begging to be included at the cool-girl lunch table in middle school, I didn't realize that one of my future best friends was sitting at a table on the other side of the room. I was going where I wanted to belong, not looking around for the spaces that God could've been leading me to. While I was wasting my time hoping these girls, whom I had nothing in common with, would include me, good things were waiting for me. When Jesus is your friend and you consistently pray for His guidance, you will get this gift called discernment. I joke that we women have "girl gut," the power of the female intuition. However, discernment is even more powerful. It leads you to truth and stops you from trusting delusions that will only lead you astray. If I'd had more discernment in my middle school years, maybe the Holy Spirit would've led me to my future best friend even sooner.

Discernment is tricky in our social media–obsessed, social-climbing world. Yet it is crucial. There's a man in the Bible named Job who was basically a good guy, called "blameless and upright"[2] by God. Satan assumed that Job only worshipped God and trusted Him because of his prosperity. God allowed Satan to cause havoc in Job's life—not because He wanted Job to experience havoc but because He knew Job's faith was strong enough and would be an example to others, including us thousands of years later. So chaos came Job's way. He lost all his property, his children died, and he suffered physically. And then his friends turned on him.

At the beginning, they did comfort him, but after a while they inaccurately described God's view of him. Job's friends belittled him in a time of great stress, grief, and pain. They made him feel worse. Job even told them, "You are miserable comforters, all of you!"[3]

I can look back on my life and see that some friends were miserable comforters. But often, I wasn't as blameless and upright as Job. Job's faith prepared him for the chaos he would face. Job knew his friends weren't being helpful, and it hurt. But he was able to discern that they were miserable comforters and not truth tellers.

Now, you and I, we have to discern when friendships are good and challenging and, like Job realized, when they aren't from God.

Miserable comforters today may not be friends who blame you when your life is chaotic, like Job's friends did. They might be more like this:

The frenemy. This is the one in your close circle who doesn't seem to support you. They almost seem happy when things don't work out for you. They call themselves a friend, but they appear to cheer against you more than for you.

The social-climbing friend. They like what you can give them but don't really know you. In groups, you wonder if they have forgotten about you. They drop your name when convenient but aren't afraid to leave you out if it means they can have something better.

The gossiping friend. They always gossip with you, but if you're being honest, you don't feel like your name is safe in rooms you aren't in. Their gossip causes you to be bitter and cynical toward others.

The ghoster friend. This friend often disappears and doesn't respond for long periods of time, not necessarily because they're going through something but because they don't feel like responding. They don't prioritize communication and clarity, leaving you confused and frustrated, constantly wondering if they even care.

These types of friends are common, and some names might even come to your mind. But the truth is, we have all been these friends at times. We need discernment not only to know which friends to lean into but also to take stock of our own behavior and know what character traits to grow and what to trim. We can be better, and we should strive to discern how to do so.

To me, the best part about Job's story is when God stuck up for him and expressed anger that Job's friends hadn't spoken the truth about God's ways.[4] So often we think we have to get even, speak our minds, and tell everyone off. But God is fighting for us. God will deal with those who tear His followers down. Trust God to fight your battles with you.

See, when Jesus was on this earth, His friends never called Him a "miserable comforter." They called Him "Teacher,"[5] and in Isaiah's prophecy about Jesus's coming, He was also referred to as "Wonderful Counselor" and "Prince of Peace."[6] A teacher is patient with someone and points them to be better, and a counselor is kind enough to listen and empathize with them. We all can be better friends.

Discernment will help you and me see where we can be better and how we can cultivate better friendships. Jesus confidently and consistently chose discernment, peace, and gentle empathy in His friendships. In Jesus, we see someone who was always the better friend. His friends let Him down, many scattered in His final moments, and one betrayed Him in the worst way. Jesus knew He was the better friend. But Jesus always showed unreasonable grace and love.

Jesus knew He was the better friend. But Jesus
always showed unreasonable grace and love.

In this book, you'll see very clearly that I am not saying you have to put up with hard, shallow, or one-sided friendships. In fact, the bravest and best thing you may do after reading this book is walk away from some friendships. However, I do want you to see that when you care more, love radically, *and* trust wisely, you will hold holy relationships that bring you peace and joy. When you live a holy life, you won't find perfect friendships, but you'll find caring comforters, genuine cheerleaders, and loving fellowship—friends who see you and care for you. We can learn from Job to identify the miserable comforters in our lives and from Jesus to become more like Him when we are the ones who can love more.

truth 2

community is created, not found

Well, here we go. I had been praying about moving to Atlanta for six months, and now I was finally doing it.

Of course, a big move meant leaving the great life I had built in Orlando. Orlando had received me as a wide-eyed twenty-two-year-old overthinking first dates and learning how to cook (I burned a lot of dishes). Orlando saw me get laid off from a job I had put my all into, and it saw me hop around friend groups trying to find my place.

But I felt like there was something more for me in Atlanta. The move made sense for my career, and it felt like a shinier city. I knew maybe two people who lived there, but God just kept putting that city on my heart. No matter what I did, I kept thinking about it. I debated for months whether the idea was really from God or just a weird obsession with *The Real Housewives of Atlanta.*

I talked to my community, friends, and mentors as well as wise women who had known me for years. Yes, I was praying about this decision, but they were too. Hearing their wisdom, advice, and stories about moving helped me discern that this transition was from God. I also researched cute apartments and prepared to rent my cute house with the pink door in Orlando, and then I moved. My parents were worried—and if I'm being honest, so was I.

It is scary to pick up everything and move to a new city, a new state. But I did it because I knew there was something more in store for me.

No one really tells you it's up to you to create community. I quickly realized this after I moved and spent my first weekend alone. I got takeout sushi, set up my television on my own (surprisingly), and watched *Friends* episodes for the fifteenth time. Phoebe was making me laugh and Joey was doing his "How you doin'?" when suddenly I looked around at my shoebox apartment with very little furniture and realized that I needed to make friends, not just watch *Friends*. I needed to actually go outside and start some conversations.

I was lonely.

We so easily believe the myth that feeling lonely is bad. Loneliness can be a lie from the Enemy to distract us and make us feel isolated from God-given people and our community. Or loneliness can be a signal from God that we need community. Loneliness reminds us that community is a primary need and that when we desire to find people, we are becoming more like God. See, something beautiful about God is that as an eternal, perfect being, He is both utterly alone, separate, and holy and, at the same time, wholly and joyfully in relationship within the Trinity. God is satisfied and complete both alone and in His triune relationship—yet He yearns for our hearts.

Loneliness reminds us that community is a primary need and that when we desire to find people, we are becoming more like God.

In Genesis 2:18, God said, "It is not good for the man to be alone." God created us and knew we needed good relationships, so He gave us the joyful opportunity to cultivate community. And God can use loneliness to remind us that He's made us for more connection. My loneliness that day, eating takeout and watching reruns, was actually a good thing. It prompted me to get out of my apartment and find new friendships.

After realizing that my weekends are not good if spent all alone, I decided I needed to meet new people. But making friends as an adult—or honestly, at any age—is hard. The main reason is that it usually involves awkward beginnings and going places alone. And as much as I wished friends would just show up at my doorstep, I knew that nothing good comes easily and that few things that are easy are also good.

Here's what I did to start my hunt for community:

1. i went to church.

At first, I went alone. I tried multiple churches until I found one I wanted to be part of, and in this process, I often sat alone. Every now and then, I would learn of a friend of a friend who also went to that church, and I would awkwardly ask to sit with them. I also looked at the Bible studies and serving opportunities available.

Let me be completely honest with you: Attending church alone was hard. A lot of churches overlook single adults. You can easily find childcare and young married groups, but it is often tough to find a Bible study that isn't for couples or that isn't closed off to new people because it's full of well-known church attendees. I would love to tell you that I walked into a church and immediately felt included. But that's not what happened. It took time.

I didn't feel like I belonged at my church until I offered to serve as a counselor for sixth-grade girls at a youth winter retreat. And through camp food, serving, early mornings, and late nights, I got to know not only sweet preteen girls but also other young adults who were serving in the youth ministry. So if you're single and trying to get active in a church, I recommend doing these three things:

Give it time, and give grace to yourself and others. Young married couples may not know what it is like to go to church alone, but others at your church do. Community takes time. No one understands your situation fully, but if you become the bold one and ask someone to meet you for lunch or coffee, you can help each other see a different perspective. Give yourself grace if you feel nervous and stumble over words when the preacher says to greet those around you. And give yourself grace in those times when you just sit in the back and try to avoid eye contact. The awkward beginnings do not mean that *you* are awkward. Sometimes these settings are uncomfortable because of a lack of consideration for single people.

Find a way to serve. Service brings people together. Ask to serve on the greeting team, in the kids ministry, in the youth ministry—anywhere in the church where you can use your gifts. I met my two good friends through serving in the youth ministry. God rewards His faithful children with blessings. Serving leads to blessings in both your life and others' lives.

Ask someone at the church what Bible study you can join. Sometimes it isn't clear what group is open to you, and it helps the church serve and care for you when you are willing to ask. Would it be better if they provided a clearer path for finding community? Yes. But if they haven't, ask for clarity. I did this after waiting months and finally got connected to a group of girls in a similar stage as mine. No one told me about this group initially; I had to seek it out. And I'm glad I did.

Give your church a chance and time. Many of us have met "friends" from church who were not kind, were cliquey, and left us out. Don't let your past hurts stop you from finding holy community today. God is doing something new.

2. i joined a gym.

Nothing brings people together more than pain—and CrossFit surely did that after I moved to Atlanta. One of my first times going, I watched everyone do handstand push-ups and thought, *Surely not everyone knows how to do this crazy gymnastic move.* I mean, I'm not Simone Biles; I'm a silly girl who writes books. But I promise you, almost everyone around me could do it. The trainer had to create an easier move for me. At first, I was embarrassed, obviously the weakest one in this class. But at the end of the class, two sweet girls around my age encouraged me and told me I did great.

It is better to show up and stumble into community than not show up at all. I still don't know how to do a handstand push-up, but those girls are cherished friends . . . and I am a little stronger. Joining a fitness class, being willing to not do so great at a new hobby, and staying a few minutes afterward to connect with others led me to community. Whether it is with a running

club, pickleball group, Pilates class, or painting club, be willing
to learn a new hobby to meet good friends.

3. i used what i could from my resources to create community.

Had I talked to my camp friend Lindsey in the last six years?
Not much. But I reached out to her once I arrived in Atlanta,
and she went out of her way to check in on me, get brunch with
me, and invite me to her favorite places. I also had dinner with
a friend of a friend, and guess what? We never saw each other
again. She was nice, but there were no friendship sparks—and
that's okay. Your resources may lead you to a forever friend or to
someone you get lunch with only once on a pretty spring day.
But it is better to try than to sit still.

4. i babysat.

I get that this doesn't sound like a community-creating tactic,
but here's the deal: I love babies and didn't have any of my
own. I asked around at my new church for anyone who needed
a babysitter. I committed only to two women I admired and
could see myself becoming friends with. I have done this in
every city I have moved to because it helps me get plugged in
to my church community in a unique way. Is changing diapers
always fun? No. I have cleaned up many blowouts and learned
not to wear a white Lululemon T-shirt to babysit an infant.
But is community found in ordinary or even unexpected
places? Oh yes. And I like to think I'm getting good practice
for when I have children—while earning money to get my
nails done.

You don't have to babysit, try a handstand push-up, or awkwardly ask a mutual friend to lunch to find community. But you do have to put yourself out there in some way, whether it's showing up to a book club, offering a skill, joining a Facebook group, or asking that girl sitting by herself at church to dinner. Remember, you won't simply stumble on community. It won't just walk up to you while you're in your pajamas in your apartment. It has to be created, initiated, encouraged, and sought after.

It is not good for you to be alone, so when you feel lonely, don't become sad. Let God remind you it is better to be with people.

types of friends

Aristotle was a Greek philosopher in the fourth century B.C., long before group text messages and avocado toast, and I have always admired his wisdom on friendship. In his book *The Nicomachean Ethics,* he classified three types of friendship:

- friendship of utility or necessity
- friendship of pleasure
- friendship of goodness[1]

Friendships can be one or any combination of these—but we must remember that our friendships of goodness are the best. Those are the friends who lead us to becoming better.

Friendships of *utility or necessity* are often the type you form with classmates, neighbors, co-workers, the fellow dog mom you meet at the park every Tuesday after work, and even the cousins you see during the holidays. These are the friends who you need to foster peace and enjoyment in your environments. In college, I worked for the football division of Baylor Athletics. Our crew of student staff worked weekend game days and prepared for recruiting events during the week. Since our boss was named Sam, our group chat was called "Sam's Soldiers." Nothing establishes friendships faster than a funny group chat name. Many of these co-working friendships became utility friendships. Some of those co-workers really got on my nerves or even hurt my feelings, yet I had to be friendly because I saw them almost daily. But Emma, who started as a colleague and friend of necessity, quickly became a friend of goodness. We went from co-workers to "Hey, I'm going to Chick-fil-A before work; do you want anything?" to hanging out together on weekends to her inviting me to her wedding.

A friend of necessity can transform into a friend of goodness. But if someone is *only* a friend of necessity, don't share everything with them or become disappointed if you're not always invited out, cherished, or made better by them. Although they can add joy to your day, oftentimes they don't know you or God enough to speak into your life with wisdom. Trust them carefully, but love them radically. God placed them in your life for a reason.

Friendships of *pleasure* are often those formed around fun experiences and shared hobbies, activities, groups, or clubs. These relationships are typically lighthearted and easygoing but not always wise. A lot of my gym friends and even my Monday night *Bachelor*-watching girl gang are friends of pleasure. Ah, nothing is more fun than watching girls cry over a boy on national television with your girls.

Friendships of pleasure are good for your soul and your physical and mental health. While they can become friendships of goodness, many simply stay friendships of pleasure. You must be aware of this so you don't become devastated when these friends break promises, share confessions that were meant to be private, or flirt with your ex-boyfriend . . . even though that sucks. I've been there.

A lot of young women have "party friends." These are the rowdy ones you may go out with but don't trust. I would encourage anyone reading this to identify your party friendships and seek to make them about something more pleasurable than getting drunk. I love margaritas with the girls, but if a friendship is only centered on going out and buying multiple drinks, chances are good there's a fallout waiting to happen. Being consistently drunk adds confusion to our lives, and confusion is never pleasurable or good.

Confusion is never pleasurable or good.

One time, I went to my going-out friends after struggling with a breakup. They gave me the best advice they knew: "To get over a guy, you gotta get under another one." Everyone laughed, and they pushed me to go out that night. I didn't get under anyone, but I did kiss a random guy. Yet I felt worse, not better. I felt like an object, and I didn't receive comfort—I received a hangover headache and cringey texts from a guy I will never see again. Friends of pleasure might surprise you, but they're typically not the best places to go when you're mourning, grieving, doubting, or sad.

Friends of *goodness* are the ones you can count on to give you sound advice, make you better, and keep your private confessions to themselves. Will they still disappoint you at times? Of course. They are human, and we live in a broken world. Will they care if they disappoint you? Yes. Friends of goodness care about you, about your Creator, and about what breaks your heart. Your relationship with them makes you better, and these friends are better than any other type. With a friendship of goodness, you get to both receive and share good—because to have a friend of goodness, you must be one. These friendships develop as you listen and care. Your bond might have started as a friendship of necessity or pleasure, but it grows to be anchored by something deeper than a hobby, an exercise class, or a job.

I think we often forget the differences between friends of necessity, pleasure, and goodness. We get disappointed with the community we have created and think we are lonely, when, truthfully, we are missing a friendship in one of these three categories.

We started this book with one of my favorite Bible verses on friendship, but I want us reflect on it again as we think about friends of goodness: "A friend loves at all times, and a brother is born for a time of adversity."[2] Your friends of goodness are meant for all times, all seasons, and all challenges.

Here are four signs your friends are friends of goodness:

- You leave your interactions together feeling peace and confidence in each relationship.
- You share kind and true words with one another, which makes you feel good and points you to your good God. Instead of empty, shallow compliments, these relationships are built on foundations of deep knowledge of one another as well as encouragement that challenges you to continue displaying the fruit of the Spirit: "love, joy, peace, patience, kindness, goodness, faithfulness, gentleness, and self-control."[3]

- You confess your sins to one another, and your friends are trustworthy with your weaknesses. They know they are not perfect but do their best to care for you both when you're in the room and when you're not.
- You give permission and trust to these friends. They may serve as your personal "board of directors." Whether you have one trusted friend or several, each one speaks life, truth, and wisdom into your decisions. They kindly make their opinions and expertise known, and they hope to lead the "business" to success. You're in the business not of achieving profit, popularity, or success but of being purposeful. Your friends of goodness help you make sound decisions that lead you to the most purposeful you. Friendships of goodness help you grow and contribute goodness to our broken world. These friends know Jesus and seek to know you well.

Friendships of goodness take patience and initiative. As I noted before, loneliness reminds us that we were not made to do life alone. I used to feel weird for trying hard to be people's friend, but then I realized other people are lonely too. Now I never hesitate to ask the new girl at Pilates to lunch or invite all my friends over for dinner on a random Tuesday. You will never be fully known if you don't first know yourself enough to admit you're lonely and do something about it. And knowing the difference between friends of goodness, necessity, and pleasure can save you from disappointment. You can learn to love them all radically but trust wisely.

Pray for your community, and pray for the eagerness to create it. Pray for patience in friendships and unexpected hellos when you boldly step out.

7 reminders
about finding and keeping friends of goodness

In his book NICOMACHEAN ETHICS, Aristotle talks about how friendship takes time to develop, inspiring this more modern take on his thoughts on friendship: "Wishing to be friends is quick work, but friendship is a slow-ripening fruit."[4] Friendship not only takes patience but also requires initiative and awkward hellos.

If you're anything like me, you get a little socially anxious...Okay, make that very socially anxious. Maybe it is because I have been left out before or because I was severely bullied in middle school, but before I meet new people, I start hearing lies like these:

- *You're going to talk too much and say the wrong thing.*
- *They don't want to be your friend. Why are you even trying?*
- *You should just stay home. This is a waste of time.*

Yet even if it doesn't work out and I don't meet a best friend while putting myself out there, I know it is better to try. God sees your efforts and will tend to your needs when you seek to grow friendships the way He created them. Trying shows your desire for deeper friendship, which points to Christ at work in you. So here are seven reminders about finding and maintaining your friends of goodness:

1. First, look around at who is in your life right now. Even if it's a friend of necessity or pleasure, see if they have the characteristics you would want in a deeper friendship.

When I was in a lonely season after moving to Orlando and feeling like everyone had a cute girl group to post about, I knew I needed to make a change. At first, I thought I needed to knock on doors and immediately find some friends. But then I remembered a girl I used to work with whom I hadn't seen in a while. She had said she, too, was a believer, and I saw kindness in how she treated me and others. After I reached out to her for more-intentional time, we hung out and she slowly became a friend of goodness.

2. Ask genuine questions of potential friends and current acquaintances. You might need to make small talk at first with the basic questions: What's your job? What's your major? Are you dating anyone? Where do you live? The answers to those questions may explain who the person is, but they don't explain why. When you follow up with detailed questions, you learn their heart and faith, not just their facts. Example questions include these: What has been your favorite age so far, and why? What can I be actively praying for in your life? Would you say you're a glass-half-full or glass-half-empty person?

3. Enjoy mundane tasks together. Oftentimes, we don't develop deep friendships of goodness because we are too busy. What a shame that is! If you're going to the grocery store, invite a friend to do their shopping with you. If you're already cooking dinner that night, text a couple of friends and see who wants to show up. One of my friends has multiple children yet still cares for me well. Our best conversations take place while she does laundry and I

kind of help but am mainly there to catch up on our lives. Sometimes growing a friendship is as simple as inviting a friend into your day-to-day and not adding anything new. You don't need to have a perfect living room that looks like no one actually lives there. You don't need to wipe every counter and spritz essential oils. Stop seeking to be put together, and instead seek to *be* together. There's nothing wrong with freshening up your house and making it feel nice, but don't become so stressed with trying to be perfect that you miss out on genuine friendships that were meant to meet you in your mess.

4. Confess your sins, both against each other and against God. Don't make it a big deal, but make it a holy habit in your friendship. If you confess to one another regularly and habitually, you're walking in the light together and avoiding the dark. Admit even a small lie, insecurity, or doubt so that confessing is part of your friendship routine, not a big, jaw-dropping moment. For me personally, in my twenties this looked like confessing my drinking habits. I was scared that my friend would judge me. She didn't drink and seemed to never make a mistake, but instead of judging, she reminded me of both God's grace and her love for me. She then regularly checked in on me. Confession within Christian community is a demonstration of God's grace and conviction, our desire to be better, and our love for one another. When I was drinking too much without telling anyone, it only became worse. If no one knows, it's hard to grow. Find friends who care for you well by listening to your confessions and encouraging you toward better choices.

As a friend, I also needed to learn to listen and cheer on confession. One summer a friend was having a hard time with an eating disorder, and I would regularly listen to her confession about how she was doing. I also had to listen and look for signs that confession was needed. Listening wasn't just about hearing her say words; it was about remembering what she had told me before and recognizing how her current actions showed she was struggling. Listen to your friend's confession, and pay attention to their actions so you care for them well.

5. There is power when two or more believers pray together. Remember that your friendship with another believer has the power to not only make you feel seen but also make you more aware of God's presence. Pray before a meal, pray while folding laundry or tucking the kids into bed, and remember that when you gather in God's name, the Holy Spirit is there. Matthew 18:19–20 says, "Again, truly I tell you that if two of you on earth agree about anything they ask for, it will be done for them by my Father in heaven. For where two or three gather in my name, there am I with them." Our Father can work wonders when we get together, so seek to be together in His name often—not just to grow your friendship but also to see miracles happen.

6. Celebrate all things, not just getting married, having babies, and buying houses. Celebrate your friend's decision to block her ex-situationship or to walk away from a job that was draining her. Holy and good friends cheer for each other to have purposeful lives, not the American

dream. Yes, rejoice in the good things, including the wedding, the baby, and the condo—but remember: Celebrating all things reminds us of the God who uses all things for our good. Friends who celebrate all things together truly see one another.

7. When you feel like a friend of goodness has failed you, ask for clarity. Explain your feelings, and never make assumptions. One time in college, I saw on a girl's phone that my friends had a group text without me. I immediately started crying and assuming it was an anti-Grace group text. Part of me wanted to block them and never trust them again. When I reluctantly approached my best friend about this anti-Grace group text, she laughed. I couldn't believe it! Here I was, crying on a Tuesday afternoon because they hated me, and she was laughing. Then she explained that they were actually trying to plan a surprise half-birthday party for me. Since I had a summer birthday, we could never celebrate together because we were always home. I remember instantly feeling so silly. My assumptions were lying to me. Seek clarity instead of jumping to conclusions in friendships.

the better friend challenge

Community is something you have to create.

- How has loneliness prompted you to seek out the relationships God made you for?

- Consider the three types of friends—friends of necessity, pleasure, and goodness—and reflect on which category each of your current friends fits into. Which category would you like to add friends to?

- How many opportunities do you have to make more friends of goodness? Do you have friends of necessity and pleasure who could become friends of goodness?

truth 3

give grace, not excuses

For a season in my life, I was part of a girl group that always had cool plans, took pretty pictures together, and was well-liked in our community. It looked fun on the outside, but if I'm honest, the group was confusing. I never knew whether they really liked me or not. Maybe you have been there too. Sure, you're invited to cute parties, and maybe you are in some photos. But every now and then, you hear a snide comment, you're not invited to random get-togethers, and you have a weird feeling they're talking about you. I couldn't tell whether these girls' jokes about me were just sarcasm or bullying.

I'll never forget when one of the girls was talking about a date she had been on. I had always been the least experienced one when it came to dating. Another girl we'll call Kimberly looked at me and said, "Well, we all know Grace hasn't even made eye contact with a guy in God knows how long."

Everyone laughed.

Except me.

The joke didn't stop there, though. Kimberly continued to talk about how everyone needed to get me drunk and take me to a bar so I could "get some."

Everyone laughed again.

Except me.

One of my insecurities was being the single friend and feeling like everyone had more experience, had more expertise, and received more attention than I did. After this conversation, I approached Kimberly and said, "Hey, I felt hurt when you made those comments about me not having much experience and poked fun saying I needed to get some. I know it wasn't your intention, but it hurt my feelings." While I said this, tears were forming in my eyes. I was doing my best to not cry because I didn't want to seem sensitive. I mean, if Kimberly was making fun of me for my inability to talk to guys, then surely she would make fun of me for crying about her "joke." And I was right.

Kimberly said, "Oh my goodness, I was joking! I forget how sensitive you are. It was not a mean comment, just a joke. I won't joke with you again then."

See, I love jokes. I like to think I can take a joke. And I wasn't trying to be sensitive—I was confused, hurt, and waiting for an apology that wasn't coming.

The next day, that group of friends went to brunch without me, maybe because they thought I couldn't take a joke. After seeing the picture on Instagram of the brunch I wasn't invited to, I felt hurt at first but then relieved. For the first time, I realized that if I had been invited, I might've been miserable and ended the night with teary eyes and confusion about whether I was even wanted. I had been fighting to feel included and loved by this group, yet when I got invited, I wasn't even happy. And when I was hurt, I would wait for an apology from people who didn't desire to grow.

Maybe we shouldn't want to be friends with people who don't respect us enough to listen to our hurts. Perhaps we shouldn't entertain constant confusion in friendships. If I don't know whether I'm considered a friend, maybe I should just find peace that I'm probably not.

Two years after this incident, I was talking to a best friend I had met at church. She made a comment about me, and I later approached her in private to say her words had hurt my feelings. Without hesitation, she apologized and asked me for forgiveness. She didn't call me sensitive; she listened.

Not long after that, a different friend was hurt by something I said. I felt awful, and I quickly apologized to her. I didn't just brush over her hurt.

Friends listen. Friends give grace.

I had a crush on a guy once, but I could never tell whether he had a crush on me. In your twenties, you kind of assume that if a guy likes you, he'll tell you or ask you on a date. However, my single girls reading this know that sometimes we play stupid, confusing games. He and I both played this game where there would be a super flirty text, some weird emoji, and then a remark about "our friendship."

I tried to play it chill. I worked on not "reading into things"— which lasted for a week. Then I began to overthink, overread, and feel confused because I kept responding to his texts and entertaining his lack of clarity.

Finally, I knew I'd had enough; I needed to figure out what he was thinking. But instead of asking for clarity, I did what many girls do who are confused by a guy: I sent about ten screenshots of our text messages to my girl group so they could analyze the conversations with me. A group project, you could say. They asked for more screenshots, and finally, the girls had three simple questions: "How many times does he text you first? Has he said anything else flirty? Do you even like him?"

In response to their simple questions, I typed out a two-paragraph analysis of how many times he had texted me first. I think I started off with "He texts me first 70% of the time." Then the rest of the reply was me deep diving into how flirty he usually was, what emojis and witty one-liners he used, and how we interacted in person. I said I could see myself liking him but was more confused, and I just needed to know how he felt. A minute or two after I sent the text, I came back to the conversation and realized something devastating: I hadn't sent this long analysis to the girls. I had sent it to *him.*

Imagine the guy opening a new text to read, "He texts me first 70% of the time" and then another two paragraphs of me scrutinizing his emoji usage and more.

I quickly unsent the message, but then the spiraling began. *Did he see the text message? It does say "Grace Valentine unsent a message" in our thread, so why hasn't he asked what I unsent? He must know.* I googled and asked more friends and discovered that apparently if he had an Apple Watch, he'd still get the text message even if I unsent it. I stalked his social media to see if he was ever pictured wearing an Apple Watch. I didn't see one, so I hoped I was in the clear.

To make things worse, I had to see him that night for a friend's birthday party. *What if he already told all the guys I sent this crazy text and they make things more awkward? What if he is standoffish and I word vomit something stupid?* I almost didn't go.

But I did go, and guess what? He was normal. Meaning, kind of flirty and still confusing. He still texted me afterward. Truthfully, though, I almost wish he had seen my fateful text, because I was seeking clarity.

Confusion isn't fun. Whether it is a guy who leads you on, a class where the professor mumbles and gives pop quizzes, a job where you were never properly trained, or a "friend" who sends mixed messages, being uncertain is tiring, adds anxious thoughts, and causes stress. Confusion isn't from God.

Maybe, like me, you've felt confused by some of your friendships. You may wonder whether the other people even care, and when you try to seek clarity or honesty, you might feel dismissed or brushed off. You never have confidence in the connection because each time you hang out, something happens that makes you question whether they are even your friends.

I have noticed that nice girls who desperately want community sometimes confuse grace with excuses. We are called to give grace to all because of the grace Jesus gives us, but if we pray for wisdom, we will realize we aren't called to trust everyone. Give grace to others, but don't excuse behavior that isn't kind.

Friendship should be all of these:

Peaceful. In 1 Corinthians 14:33, the Bible says, "God is not the author of confusion, but of peace" (KJV). When I consistently felt unsure whether a friend liked or cared for me and whether I was better for their company, I'd think God was sending me a warning signal that this friend was not from Him. If a "friend" continually causes you to be confused, they are not a gift from God.

Empowering. True friends pick each other up when they fall. They lead each other to be better and aren't afraid to speak truth, even when it can be uncomfortable and hard. They let others know when they are hurt, and they receive accountability with grace and eager ears. True friends trust each other to make them better. Ecclesiastes 4:9–10 says, "Two are better than one, because they have a good return for their labor: If either of them falls down, one can help the other up. But pity anyone who falls and has no one to help them up." When you fall—when you mess up, hurt each other, make a mistake, drink too much, or kiss the wrong boy—true friends pick you up and call you higher. They don't push you down and lead you to sin, teary eyes, and hurt.

Kind. True friends share words of kindness, not gossip or hurtful words. They speak well of each other and others. When kind and gracious words surround you, you become better and your body and soul are healthier. The Mayo Clinic found that kindness can "decrease blood pressure and cortisol, a hormone directly correlated with stress levels." And people who show kindness and encouragement "tend to be healthier and live longer."[1] Proverbs 16:24 says, "Kind words are like honey—sweet to the soul and healthy for the body" (NLT).

Walking away from friendships that consistently tear you down can feel weird when you're the girl who tries to be nice all the time. But Jesus didn't call us to be nice; He called us to be faithful, kind, loving, and gentle and to show self-control. Kindness still shares truth and is loving enough to confront someone if they are unintentionally or intentionally hurting others. Often, when we are trying to be nice, we excuse behaviors that are confusing, belittling, and hurtful—that lead us away from God's goodness. In fact, sometimes we try so hard to be nice that we don't make our friends better or find better friends. Friendship should bring peace, empowerment, and kindness.

*Sometimes the kindest thing we can do is walk away
from someone who is pushing us away from God's
goodness.*

Sometimes the kindest thing we can do is walk away from someone who is pushing us away from God's goodness. When we entertain and excuse their continual teardowns, we are letting them live an unkind life unchecked, which can lead them to hurt themselves and others. Friends push friends to be better; they don't allow their friends to hurt others without question.

Don't accept behavior from others that makes you doubt your worth, steals your peace, and hurts your heart. You might have the discernment to realize that an unkind friend is belittling you because of their own insecurity, hardships, and doubt. However, just because something explains their actions doesn't mean you have to excuse them.

Friendships are a powerful source of joy, peace, and comfort, but when you give that role to a group of people or a person who isn't seeking to make you better, the relationship can be poison. It is better to be lonely than surrounded by people who make you feel belittled.

*It is better to be lonely than surrounded by people
who make you feel belittled.*

7 truths
for loving radically but trusting wisely

When I started online dating, I texted my best friends, "I'm going to share my location, and here's a screenshot of the guy's profile who I'm meeting up with. I'm meeting him at this restaurant. This is for you to have just in case he kidnaps me and I go missing. Thanks! Wish me luck."

Ah, thank you to all my friends who tracked me while I was meeting up with strangers! But I chuckle when I think about what I expected of them. I trusted that if I didn't text that I was home safe by 10:00 P.M., they would track my location, show up to the restaurant, corner the server to find out when and where I was last seen, get a dog to track my scent, and find me before the internet man could sneak me out of the country. I know my friend Mckenzie would've done all the above, plus gotten my picture on the news, and she would've known which pictures of me were the good ones.

I trusted my friends to flip the world over if I disappeared. I trusted my friends to care. And knowing I could trust them gave me peace of mind.

Trust is powerful and crucial in friendships. Trust in the right hands makes you feel seen and known and safe, and it makes your relationships vibrant. But trust that is reckless or placed in the wrong people can lead to pain and hurt. Many of us have had our trust broken, and that is one of the worst feelings we can experience. Being let down by someone we thought was our friend causes us grief. We grieve the person we thought we knew and had our back.

However, though we should be wise about trusting others, we should also love radically. Christ laid down His life for us, and we are called to die to ourselves and be the ones who love in big ways in this broken world. I think we are so scared of looking pathetic and being taken advantage of that we forget Jesus modeled radical love. He loved us while we were yet sinners. Now over two thousand years later, you and I are troubled about being the better friends. I am here to say we can be both radically loving and wisely trusting. We give everyone love and grace because of the Cross, but trust comes from wisdom and discernment. We should love all and trust few in order to experience vibrant and fulfilling friendships and to honor Jesus's love for us.

Remember these seven truths about loving radically but trusting wisely:

1. Trust comes from discernment, and discernment comes through prayer. If you want to figure out whom to trust, invite God to help you discern. Ask for the Holy Spirit to guide you. James 1:5 says, "If any of you lacks wisdom, you should ask God, who gives generously to all without finding fault, and it will be given to you." When we ask for wisdom, God gives it to us. So why don't we ask for His wisdom to guide our friendships?

2. Luke 6:35–36 says, "Love your enemies, do good to them, and lend to them without expecting to get anything back. Then your reward will be great, and you will be children of the Most High, because he is kind to the ungrateful and wicked. Be merciful, just as your Father is merciful." Sometimes we want to become bitter and feel hurt when we love someone better and care more than they do. Yet we

give grace, not excuses   37

are called to do good to all, including our enemies, without expecting anything in return. The reward comes from being a blessing and living out a love that reflects the love of Christ.

3. Your kindness and radical love say more about your God than about you or your friends. Being kind doesn't make you pathetic. In fact, when looking back at your interactions, wouldn't you rather be the kinder one? Isn't that something to be proud of? Show kindness gladly, and remember it will show others your Savior's love. Matthew 5:16 says, "Let your light so shine before men, that they may see your good works, and glorify your Father which is in heaven" (KJV). Know that your love is a gift not only to others but also to your God and to yourself. You are being a light, not being pathetic. When you know God's character and Word, you discern that your love is a gift, not a burden.

4. You become a more attractive friend when you live life unoffendable and assume the best. Friends hung out without you? You will be okay. Pitching a fit doesn't show what actually makes you a good friend to others. People want to surround themselves with those who bring them peace, not those who bring assumptions. Throw away your entitlement. Know the difference between jumping to conclusions and being discerning. If we feel left out, discernment may reveal a deeper issue in our hearts, but insecurity may cause us to jump to conclusions and assume the worst. Never do that. Listen to discernment, not assumptions based on your sense of entitlement.

5. Even though it is good to assume the best, we must remember it is foolish to continually trust someone who has shown us their untrustworthy character. If a person isn't walking in a holy manner, be aware that their advice won't point you to your true purpose. Non-Christian friends can give good advice but never holy advice. It is crucial as a Christian for you to surround yourself with friends who will point you to God and your true purpose.

6. You don't need to seek revenge. Walk away from friendships where there is betrayal or no trust. But trust that God will defend you as His child. If someone continually hurts people, God will deal with them. It is not your job to seek revenge, tell the town, and seek their punishment. Romans 12:19 says, "Do not take revenge, my dear friends, but leave room for God's wrath, for it is written: 'It is mine to avenge; I will repay,' says the Lord." It is easy to want to shout it from the rooftops when someone hurts you, but remember to "leave room for God's wrath" because it is more powerful than any revenge you could seek.

7. You will fail your friends, and you probably have failed an ex-friend. Remember, God's grace is more powerful than anything you have done, but it is your responsibility to grow. God makes you new, but living in sin makes you a bad friend. No one will want to be trustworthy to you if you don't first walk in a manner worthy of trust.

*You become a more attractive friend when you live
life unoffendable and assume the best.*

the better friend challenge

· Do any of your current friendships constantly leave you
feeling confused, belittled, or hurt? Identify these friendships, and ask God to give you wisdom to discern whether
you need to have a conversation or walk away from them.

· What does it mean to give grace to others but not excuse
unkind behavior?

Write a prayer for your friendships. Ask God to give you
grace to forgive those who have hurt you and discernment to
recognize untrustworthy friendships.

truth 4

comparison kills community

In the college house I shared with four other girls, I went upstairs one afternoon to see two of my roommates in the bathroom getting ready for a fraternity formal. They were curling their hair, painting mascara on their eyelashes, and swapping pretty dresses. They both had dates for the fancy dinner while I still didn't know how to talk to a boy without yapping about Taylor Swift. Both of these friends were better with guys than I was, and I often compared myself to them.

Do boys like them better because they are hotter? Maybe it's because they are funnier than me.

Both of them also had more expensive makeup. *Maybe if I could afford better makeup and fancy dresses, I would be asked to the fraternity formal.*

They are going to have so much fun tonight! They'll become closer friends and have a more exciting college experience than me.

Dramatic, right? They got one invite to a fraternity formal, and suddenly I found myself feeling ugly, boring, and left behind.

*Comparison highlights another's best while only
allowing you to see your worst.*

My spiraling thoughts didn't make sense, but that's typical
with comparison. Comparison highlights another's best while
only allowing you to see your worst. And when you compare
yourself to someone else, you can make an enemy out of a
friend.

In comparing myself to my roommates, I wasn't being a good
friend to them and I was not kind to myself. I distanced myself
from them, began to think negative thoughts, and didn't care for
them well—all because I was envious.

What's ironic is that night while they were at the fraternity
formal—having fun, taking cute pictures, and dancing the night
away—I was writing for my blog, a little website that helped me
get my first book deal. All of us were right where we needed to
be. I wasn't missing out. Maybe I wasn't asked to the big event
because I was awkward at flirting and not good with boys. Yet it
didn't matter, because God had His hand over each of our lives.
I wasn't meant to live the same life they were, but I was meant
to cheer them on.

Five years later, I facetimed one of those best friends who
had attended the fraternity formal. She was happily married to
someone other than her date that night and caring for her two
babies. I was an author, still learning how to date and giggling
with her about a first date with a cute guy I had connected with
online. I had gone on many first dates with guys I met online,
and Britta heard about every single one. Both of us had grown
up and realized that God's hand was over our lives. We weren't

meant to have each other's blessings, but we were meant to have each other.

Comparison creates division and kills community.

Sometimes it is hard to remember there is no one correct timeline for life. I confessed to a newer friend one day that I was comparing myself to her since she met her husband so young, drove a nice car, made cute dinners for her husband, and seemed to be ahead of me. She laughed and admitted that she had actually been struggling to not compare herself to me, feeling behind in her creative career and wishing she had started younger like I did.

God placed us both in the middle of a blessing, but all we could do was look at each other's blessings and compare gifts. If we waste time looking at what God is giving someone else, we will miss out on the blessings God has provided for us.

If we waste time looking at what God is giving someone else, we will miss out on the blessings God has provided for us.

My singleness was an area of my life where I struggled to feel content. I was a bridesmaid eight times and had sat through multiple baby showers. I watched my friends create beautiful families while I was living in cramped old houses with new roommates, struggling to pay bills, babysitting, and figuring out how to adult. *How can some of my friends be purposefully trying to get pregnant while I'm still babysitting for side cash?*

My comparison made me resentful. I resented my friends for so effortlessly finding love while I was putting myself out there on an app and for trying to give dating advice while not setting me up with any of their husbands' friends. That led me to start resenting God. And when I was bitter toward both my community and my God, I felt lonelier than before.

An insecure you is a bad friend. When you're insecure and jealous, you're not caring for your friends or yourself well. Proverbs 14:30 says, "A heart at peace gives life to the body, but envy rots the bones." Envy destroys your mental, physical, and social health. Envy makes you miserable and causes you to be unkind, making others miserable in return.

An insecure you is a bad friend. When you're insecure and jealous, you're not caring for your friends or yourself well.

I spent many days praying for the kind of life my friends had. I prayed for a husband and a bigger house. I prayed to be able to afford a dog and not fear any vet bills. (God knows I couldn't have afforded a dog eating my Trader Joe's Dark Chocolate Peanut Butter Cups.) Finally, I felt God convict me. He reminded me I needed to be confident in who I was and content with who I was not.

While comparison kills community, contentment creates healthy community. When you are content in who God is, confident in who He made you, and okay with what your life is not, your community can be full of life and joy instead of competition and insecurity.

Psalm 84:11 says, "The LORD God is a sun and shield; the LORD bestows favor and honor; no good thing does he withhold from those whose walk is blameless." This is a simple but powerful scripture to remember when you're seeking contentment. As we read this verse, we see five truths:

- The Lord is like the sun. The sun is what makes life on Earth possible. Goodness comes from the sun's warmth and light, just like the good in your life comes from God.
- The Lord God is our shield. He protects us. When things don't happen for you, it could very well be that God is leading you to what's really meant for you. Rejection from people in your life is likely God's protection.
- Honor and favor come from God. The Lord wants to lead you to His blessings. He doesn't want you feeling like you missed out. He doesn't promise to fulfill your plans, but He does promise you favor and honor if you trust in Him and walk with Him.
- God is not in the business of withholding good things from us. If it were good for you to have your friend's life, He would give it to you. People forget, though, that God is creative and kind enough to know what each of us needs for our good. Trust in His creativity, and care for your life more than you compare.
- It is important that our walk is "blameless." We must remember that this verse doesn't say "those whose walk is perfect" or "pretty." Our everyday should be focused on trusting God, being obedient, and being kind to others so they look at our lives as a reflection of God and not a cause of their pain.

If we remember that God is good and is good to *us*, we find peace and contentment. When we are content with our lives, we learn to celebrate our friends and the goodness in their lives. It is hard to be envious of someone when you're celebrating them well. And instead of comparing yourself to your friend, you can invite them into your life more, cheer them on as a teammate, and even learn from their life.

Instead of resenting what my friends had, I began to participate in their lives. When a friend had a baby, I took dinner over, cuddled her cute mini-her, laughed when the baby tried to breastfeed from me, and prayed over her family. Each time I went on a first date, I would call my married friends and process it over the phone. When my friend moved to a new city, I planned a trip and surprised her with flowers for her new apartment. If a friend went through a breakup, I took her cookies and ice cream, paid for the movie *John Tucker Must Die,* and listened to her while reminding her of her worth.

Instead of resenting what my friends had, I began to participate in their lives.

Invite yourself into your friends' wildly different blessings and obstacles. Care for yourself enough to give yourself grace, celebrate your current blessings, and be content with what you're not. And care for your friends enough to celebrate and comfort them when their lives look different from yours.

Some of my most treasured moments in life now are when my friends and I come together and, instead of comparing ourselves, share our present blessings and current trials. I'll never forget sitting outside a friend's house, on her cute outdoor patio with her two babies, talking about life. She was cheering me on in a season when I was traveling to speak, learning how to date, and figuring everything out. For the first time, sharing lemonade in the bright Florida sun, I realized it is way more fulfilling to cheer each other on than compare. I'm happy she got the sweet family, and if anything, I try to spoil her children. And she is happy for me. Being a part of your friends' lives reminds you that God's hand is over all His children.

I don't want to waste any more time longing for what isn't for me. I hope you and I can be fully confident and content so we can uniquely celebrate our friends. May we remember we are called to be teammates, not competitors. May we walk blamelessly and trust that God does not withhold good from us. Let's be confident in our own God-given lives and invite our friends into them too. Let's strive to be content in God's goodness and expectant of God's favor to walk with us each day.

7 reminders
about comparison

I went nineteen years of my life eating sandwiches normally. I would add meat, maybe some lettuce, and some cheese; I'd lightly toast the bread (of course), and it would be great. I thought that was as good as a sandwich could get. Then in college, I saw my friend and roommate Dresden do something crazy: She put Kettle Brand Sea Salt Chips on her sandwich, literally right in the middle. I remember saying something like "Ew, why did you put chips in your sandwich?"

She chuckled and explained she once saw a friend do it, then tried it and enjoyed it. Now she does it every time. I laughed at how silly chips on a sandwich sounded, but a week later, I was eating a sandwich at the dining hall and noticed there were chips by the sandwich bar. That day, inspired by Dresden, I put chips on my sandwich. Now almost ten years later, I still put chips on my sandwich. Every now and then, someone comments on it, and all I can think about is Dresden. She now lives in California, and I am on the other side of the country in Georgia, and we're both still putting chips on our sandwiches. We don't talk often anymore, but I cherish the friendship we had, and I think of her every time I get a Publix turkey sub with sea salt chips.

I could tell you more stories about how my friends have influenced me: I learned not to overdo the eyeliner from my friend Britta. I got addicted to the game *RollerCoaster Tycoon* the summer before sixth grade because whenever I went to Leah's house, we played it for four hours straight. My friend Lizzy drove me around in her Volvo, and five years later, I saved up money to get one of my own. When my sunroof is open and I'm jamming to Taylor Swift, I think of Lizzy. Oh, and one time I walked into Chick-fil-A and saw a girl dipping her fries in both ranch and ketchup, and ever since that day, I have used this strategy too. *Life-changing.*

Our friends, family, and even the random girl at Chick-fil-A can inspire us, show us something new, or entertain us. We can learn different hobbies and explore opportunities we'd never think possible because of someone who is in our lives for a season, a moment, or a lifetime. I think each of us looks at our friends and either becomes inspired by them or wants to be them. Being inspired is healthy and normal, but wanting to be them is sinful and unkind to you, your Creator, and your friends.

I had a close friend who called herself fat one time. She

weighed a solid twenty-five pounds less than me. I rolled my eyes at her in disbelief, but for the next five months, I compared my body to hers. We went from being close friends to me resenting her—all because comparison crept into our friendship.

Inspiration is good and fun. You can love your friend's style and adopt her love for pink sweaters or high-waisted jeans. But if you find yourself wishing you were her, you're exhausting yourself with comparison, and your friendship will suffer. Comparison isn't healthy for your peace, nor is it beneficial for your friendship. So to keep comparison out of your friendships, take these seven simple reminders to heart:

1. Ecclesiastes 1:14 says, "I have seen all the things that are done under the sun; all of them are meaningless, a chasing after the wind." Fighting to be the best and working for earthly validation is meaningless, a race with no finish line. Seek to be better in Christ's name, not better than other people in worldly titles.

2. Maybe you can't be the prettiest, smartest, or coolest girl in the room. But you can be the most inclusive and the kindest girl who brings out everyone's best. Seek to make people better, not to be the best.

3. Don't be afraid to keep some things private when interacting with a friend who tends toward jealousy. Privacy is different from secrecy. Some people in your life can't be trusted to celebrate you well. Use discernment and prayer to know whom to trust to cheer you on wholeheartedly.

4. We live in a culture that constantly prompts us to be self-obsessed or self-loathing. Instead, be self-aware. Be confident of who you are and the gifts God has given you, while also being content and okay with who you are not. You may not be the lawyer or the chill girl who so effortlessly gets all the guys. You may have a friend who is better at style or a friend who has a faster metabolism than you. That's okay. Your gifts are just as valuable. If you're too busy looking to the left and the right at everyone else and what they have, you'll miss out on the blessings God has placed right in front of you.

5. Confess your jealousy to your friends. Ask them for grace. I shared earlier how I told a new friend I was struggling with comparing myself to her and she confessed the same thing in return. Our friendship grew through that shared honesty. Speak the lies you believe so truth can enter your heart and your friendship.

6. Acts 2:44–47 says, "All the believers were together and had everything in common. They sold property and possessions to give to anyone who had need. Every day they continued to meet together in the temple courts. They broke bread in their homes and ate together with glad and sincere hearts, praising God and enjoying the favor of all the people. And the Lord added to their number daily those who were being saved." This was written when the early church was forming. The early church grew so fast because everyone recognized that church isn't a building or place; it's the people. You and your friends should be

the church. When you live a loving life, you stop wasting time convincing others you're worth loving. You're more focused on loving others well than comparing yourself to them. When you have a generous posture, you walk in God's favor and blessings. Give your neighbors your time, your attention, compliments, and a celebratory attitude. Don't covet a life that was never meant to be yours.

7. You get one life—one opportunity to live in this broken world for Jesus. When comparison lives in your heart, it prevents you from walking truly and freely in that purpose. There is no one correct timeline, so remember you're never behind when you're walking with Jesus. If you're walking with your Savior, you're walking in His best.

the better friend challenge

How has comparison shown up in your friendships? Give yourself permission to be honest about whom you have compared yourself to and why.

- How might your life and friendships look different if you became a celebrator of your friends' joys and achievements?

- How can you embrace the truth that God is not withholding any good thing from you?

Say a prayer to God, asking Him to help you and your friends invite each other into your wildly different lives.

truth 5

don't beg to sit at tables
Jesus hasn't prepared for you

"Grace Valentine has been added to the group text." I think I screamed with excitement when I got that notification. Was I a fifteen-year-old being invited into the homecoming group? Was I seventeen and finally invited to the party with the cute guys at the cool parents' house who let kids hang out without supervision (which definitely was never my high school experience)? Nope, I was a twentysomething in Atlanta a week after moving and had just been invited into a new friend group that planned great weekends, had a good girl-to-guy ratio, and was fun. I knew some people in this friend group before I moved to the city, and I wanted so badly for these friends to want me in their group. Now finally, with that text, I was officially one of them.

The group text was full of GIFs, hangout times, exciting plans, and new friendships. It was fun—for four whole business days. Then the drama happened.

Some of the friends in the group gossiped about the others. At first, I thought, *Wow, they really trust me. Everyone is venting to me. I must be everyone's safe place.* Then I realized I wasn't that special—they all talked about everyone to everyone. They didn't gossip about only each other, though; they talked badly about random people walking down the street. Their hangouts usually involved lots of alcohol, some little drunk disagreement, and more gossip, on repeat.

Here I was, finally in the group text, dealing with high-school-level drama but with more hormones, more alcohol, and a couple of disagreements. Why did this friend group I had wanted to be a part of so badly make me feel so horrible? I thought I just needed to host a girls' dinner. I invited some sweet church friends, some mutual college connections, and the girls from this rowdy friend group. *This will fix everything!*

It did not fix everything.

I made a chicken pasta and salad for everyone. I bought wine and even nice glasses. I rented out my apartment clubhouse so there would be enough room for everyone. And the girls' dinner began. We prayed over the meal, but then, instead of a light girls' night, the mix of personalities led to an evening of chaos. It wasn't the church friends or the mutual college friends; it was the group—the ones I thought were so cool—who created the trouble. They sat off to the side, whispered to one another, obviously talked about other people, and didn't speak to any of my other friends. As I watched everyone at this dinner party, I finally realized I was begging to sit at a table that Jesus never prepared for me. This was not my table to be a part of.

I had so badly wanted this group to accept me, and in return I was allowing disorder and conflict into my life. When I stopped by their group to chat for a few minutes, I heard more gossip—this time about some of my other friends in the room whom I cared deeply about. That was the moment I knew these friends were not the community God had in mind for me.

The girls' dinner was rough, but I am almost thankful I got

to see the comparison so clearly that night. Some of my friends who were there talked about life, careers, and hobbies; shared jokes; and opened up about hard situations. The other group sat there gossiping about everyone else.

While Jesus was on this earth, He had an intense encounter where He flipped some tables. Matthew 21:12–15 tells the story:

> Jesus entered the temple courts and drove out all who were buying and selling there. He overturned the tables of the money changers and the benches of those selling doves. "It is written," he said to them, "'My house will be called a house of prayer,' but you are making it 'a den of robbers.'"
>
> The blind and the lame came to him at the temple, and he healed them. But when the chief priests and the teachers of the law saw the wonderful things he did and the children shouting in the temple courts, "Hosanna to the Son of David," they were indignant.

In this passage, Jesus was calling out those who were selling in the temple courts and often scamming people. With righteous anger, He disrupted the business by flipping tables. And afterward, He again showed His power by healing everyone.

When we read this story, we can notice two things:

- Anger isn't necessarily a bad emotion. It's okay to have righteous anger. "'My house will be called a house of prayer,' but you are making it 'a den of robbers.'"[1] Jesus didn't want His house to be used for the things of this world. It was wrong. A house of prayer isn't meant to be a place for robbers. Jesus's anger was actually His holy conviction. When something doesn't sit right or seem kind, maybe this is the Holy Spirit telling us that we should have righteous anger. We should still maintain self-control and gentleness, but our anger isn't bad. In fact, it may be a holy guide.

- The Bible calls Jesus's flipping tables and then healing the lame and blind "wonderful things."[2] Sometimes the act of walking away and focusing on the tables God has prepared for you is the "wonderful thing" God is calling you to do. Like Jesus, we are meant to gracefully walk toward the tables and plans God has prepared for us.

At any age and in any stage of life, it is possible to meet people who make friendships selfish and full of chaos, drama, and gossip. I was angry at the group I first longed to be a part of because they took a wholesome dinner and made it full of drama and even hurt people they didn't know. I am glad I still had conviction from the Holy Spirit to see that the way they were treating themselves and others wasn't full of goodness or kindness. My anger was from God, and it showed me that I didn't need to stay with these friends.

Friendships are supposed to be communities of kindness, prayer, and peace, not dens where people rob joy, clarity, and love. When I participated in the group and the text conversations, I was joining the den and turning my attention away from true friendships.

Friendships are supposed to be communities of kindness, prayer, and peace, not dens where people rob joy, clarity, and love.

Walking away from that friend group was a hard but wonderful thing for me. I wanted to see God's power in my life, not worldly acceptance. After the girls' dinner, I removed myself slowly from the group. I stopped responding and eventually left the group text. I heard later that the drama only continued. More people came into the group, and others left. I'm sure there was someone else like me, excited to be added to the group text but eventually realizing this table would only steal connection. Even as adults, we can feel like middle school girls begging to fit into the girl group with the pretty Vera Bradley lunch boxes. But no joy comes from begging to be with people who will lead you away from God's goodness.

Proverbs 12:26 says, "The righteous choose their friends carefully, but the way of the wicked leads them astray." As we choose our friends, we must be careful, wise, and discerning enough to see when they are a table that the Lord never intended for us to join.

So when you meet new friends, here are things to look out for while you pray about whether this table is meant for you:

- Watch how they talk about others, their friends as well as strangers. If they constantly talk about their friends to you, they probably talk about you too.
- Watch how they talk about themselves. Obviously, we need to hold grace for everyone because we all deal with various levels of insecurity. But if the person you are befriending constantly seeks affirmation and lives in insecurity, it's a sign that they may not have the capacity to love friends well. This does not mean you have to ditch them; in fact, you should do the opposite. You should love them well, invite them into your life, and be kind. They need to be reminded that they

are loved by Jesus. However, you have to have holy boundaries and understand that a consistently insecure person seeking constant affirmation doesn't always have the ability to be the friend you may need.

• And watch how they make you feel. If you constantly feel ashamed, embarrassed, put down, or overlooked, chances are these friends are not setting a good table.

Something really beautiful about that girls' dinner party was the other friends who came. I saw two of them recently at church, and they both asked me instantly, "How's your book going? I have been praying for you." I know they are cheering me on, asking genuine questions, and when I talk with them, I feel seen, loved, honored, and cared for. Receiving their love without fear of distrust is beautiful. Theirs was a table God wanted me to sit at. And I am glad I found such a welcoming place to learn and love alongside friends who make me better.

Life isn't about having a clique. It's about knowing Jesus and finding a community, not just four best friends.

---

7 ways
to cultivate deep community
without being exclusive

Exclusivity hurts. It's never fun to feel like everyone but you is invited to a group chat, the popular lunch table, or the cool club. There was a point in my life when I was trying so hard to be everyone's friend that I wasn't a good friend to the ones I was closest to. In the process of trying to show up for everyone, I forgot one of my best friends' birthdays. That was bad. I had to apologize and remember that I didn't need a vast network of people to know me. I needed quality friendships with trusted people who had hospitable hearts.

Maybe you're like me and exclusivity has hurt you, so you go out of your way to be nice to everyone at the cost of your really good friendships. It is important for you to remember you're called to be kind, inviting, and discerning, not to be nice. *Nice* isn't a biblical word. *Nice* can easily be a fake interaction or a quick, meaningless compliment, or it can mean pretending to be someone's friend but not actually caring about them. We have so many friends on social media whom we only pretend to know. We comment, "Love ya, girl!" but we don't ever talk about anything important—or even meet.

Christ calls you to know your community, not just to know of them.

Christ calls you to have deep and meaningful relationships, not popularity with a wide group of people.

We want to have spirits that are inviting and not exclusive, because we know how hurtful exclusivity can be. Yet we also need to honor the deep relationships we have. So let's remember these seven truths.

1. Identify the difference between your "bridesmaid" friends, your "dance floor" friends, and friends who wouldn't be invited to your wedding. This sounds cheesy, but it helps me identify my true community. Your bridesmaid friends are the three to ten best friends who walk with you, who fully know you, and whom you fully know. They are the ones you're on mission with. Your dance floor friends may not know every detail about your life, but they care for you well. And the friends who aren't on the wedding invitation list are simply those whom you love well and interact with when God leads you to one another but who aren't your core community.

    I so often see women obsess over finding their best friends, but they forget to find their tribes. You need both bridesmaid and dance floor friendships. Both make you better. You can care for both groups differently but consistently. Life isn't about having a clique. It's about knowing Jesus and finding a community, not just four best friends.

2. An inviting spirit serves the overlooked well. And often when you serve, you receive more blessings than you give.

    In Acts 9, we read about a woman named Tabitha who loved Jesus, was good at sewing, and made clothes for the widows and the poor. Some may have overlooked and forgotten the poor and the widowed, but not Tabitha. She felt compelled to see them and give them clothes. When Tabitha died, messengers were sent to Peter, asking him to come, presumably to restore this beloved woman. Tabitha helped people who had nothing to give her, and in return, her community worked together to bring about her healing. Peter traveled to Tabitha's bedside and prayed, and God raised her from the dead. She was focused on loving the overlooked, not seeking approval from the popular.

There was a season in my life when I felt lonely. I knew some country club members, some people of influence, and even some "famous" people who commented on my posts. But I didn't have deep community. I started getting more involved at my church, serving teenage mothers through a program called YoungLives, and putting myself in places to love the overlooked. And the same people I came to serve, served me. When you live a loving life and care for others, you'll find a loyal community that cares for you well.

3. Sometimes to stand by your friends, you have to walk away from others. There is a Taylor Swift song that goes, "A friend to all is a friend to none."[3] You're called to be loving to everyone, but to invest your energy and time in your best friends, you may need to walk away from people who have repeatedly hurt you or them. You should want your best friends to know that you care about them more than you care about being liked by all. Don't seek affirmation; seek to love your friends well. You don't need to encourage sin, gossip, or exclusivity; and in some cases where real harm has been caused, the most loving thing you can do is walk away from someone who has hurt your friend. It isn't exclusive to stand by your friends.

4. Don't gatekeep your friendships or keep them separate. Introduce everyone. Sometimes if I know someone is seeking more close friendships but I don't have the capacity for that, I plan a group hangout with other friends I think they would thrive with. Don't keep good people away from each other. You can't be friends to all, but you can be a connector. Connect your friends to people who will help them thrive. A connecting friend is a kind friend.

5. First Corinthians 10:27 says, "If someone who isn't a believer asks you home for dinner, accept the invitation if you want to. Eat whatever is offered to you without raising questions of conscience" (NLT). We are never above sharing a meal with someone. Accept the invitations that come your way as long as you feel comfortable, safe, and purposeful in going. Always have a posture of being ready to bring the good news to those who don't know God.

   When I felt lonely, I started hosting parties at my house and would invite anyone who wanted to come. Plenty of people didn't show, and that's okay. But lots of others came and were excited to meet new people. Some were believers and some were nonbelievers. Receive invitations, and always extend invitations when you can.

6. Proverbs 19:17 says, "Whoever is generous to the poor lends to the LORD, and he will repay him for his deed" (ESV). We may tend to think generosity is just about money, but when we find community that is fulfilling, kind, and vibrant, we should share it. Loneliness makes one's life feel poor. When you live a loving life and invite the lonely in, too, goodness from God comes your way.

Karma isn't biblical, but the Lord does reward His children when they live a loving life. The repayment isn't a promotion, popularity, or a 401(k) that gets you to early retirement and a full-time pickleball lifestyle. It is hearing "Well done, good and faithful one" from our Creator and Lord. The repayment is being led to God's best while still living in this chaotic world. You will find fulfillment in a generous life.

7. Be the weird friend and neighbor. Amaze others consistently with love—whether that's surprising your friend on her birthday, driving to see a friend after she goes through a breakup, helping a friend move, or taking dinner to your neighbor. Being weirdly kind is different but good. Love is shown. It doesn't just talk. Jesus said, "By this everyone will know that you are my disciples, if you love one another."[4] Let people and your friends know you are Christian by your love. And invite your friends into the acts of kindness. Ask them to help you throw a surprise party, come with you to serve the homeless, or help out with a Bible study. When someone is grieving a loss or going through a rough time, create a Meal Train with your friends. Friends who radically love others and one another have Christ's presence in their friendship.

Remember, Jesus walked with only twelve disciples but loved many people while He was on earth. He never looked down on having dinner with someone; instead, He brought His friends into His radically loving life. Bring your friends along and be loving together. It's been said that Billy Graham once advised, "Find some friends, change the world, and have fun doing it."

Jesus never asked you to be everyone's best friend. He asked you to love everyone but not to walk this life closely with everyone or strive to be liked by everyone. Find peace in remembering Jesus can be everyone's friend and savior, even while you can't. That doesn't make you a mean person; it just means you are human.

So not every table, group text, or invite is for you. Don't beg to sit at tables that God didn't prepare for you. Be discerning, be aware, and choose your friendships wisely. A few individual, holy friendships are always better than a popular yet unkind clique. Good friendships are waiting for you, but you'll never meet them if you're too busy begging for a table that was never meant for you in the first place. Pick up your chair and walk toward God's best.

When you live a loving life and invite the lonely in, too, goodness from God comes your way.

the better friend challenge

• Have you ever desperately wanted to be friends with people who weren't good for you? If so, why did you want their approval so badly?

• When you are around friends who make you a better person, what do your conversations sound like? How do they feel?

• Have you ever met a friend whom you felt was sent from God? Why did you feel that way? Do you have any current friendships like this? If not, where might you search for this kind of friendship?

truth 6

call your friends up, not out

When I first started dating my boyfriend, Matt, I was immediately smitten. I mean, he is everything I've prayed for, can make me laugh, and has a cute dimple on his cheek—how could I not be? One of my favorite things about him is that he has good friends who love him well and whom he loves well too.

Two days after we became official, one of my best friends, Ramsey, was in town. Matt's friends had fun weekend plans, so we tagged along. After dinner, we went to a bar to watch a championship game, and as I was getting a drink, I placed my jacket and purse by a random group of three guys and asked them to watch my things. Ten minutes later, I had forgotten where I put my stuff. I had dropped my purse off to these strangers so quickly, it wasn't something I remembered. Ramsey immediately started to help me search. I like to call this hectic situation Purse-gate. Keep in mind, keys to a shiny 2023 Volvo were in this purse. (Maybe be more responsible with your stuff than I am.)

As I looked for my things, Matt came up to me and said, "Let me help. Should we go back to the restaurant? I'll call them now."

I remember thinking, *Dang, Matt has never been hotter.* He

didn't make me feel stupid for losing my purse, even though to lose it within five minutes of entering a bar was pretty pathetic. Though, if he was going to seriously date me, he would probably need to be good at finding things. It wasn't long until the three random guys I had handed my stuff to saw me searching and presented me with my purse and jacket. I bought them drinks for keeping my precious fifteen-dollar purse safe.

After Purse-gate, both Ramsey and I were so proud of the way Matt handled my hot-mess tendency. Once we got back to my apartment that night, Ramsey said, "When Matt was helping you look for your purse, that was so sweet, Grace!"

Sounds silly, but I was blushing over a guy helping me look for a purse!

Two weeks later, we were on a double date, and Matt's friend's wife told me a cute story about the boys during Purse-gate. As I said, Matt and I had been two days into dating at the time. While the football game was going on, his friends saw Ramsey and I frantically searching for my purse and said to him, "Matt, your girlfriend lost her purse."

Matt just nodded his head, watching football. "Oh dang."

His friends looked at him again. "Matt, your *girlfriend* lost her purse."

Finally, Matt understood what they were hinting at: I was his girlfriend, and he should help me. So then he sprang up and searched with me.

When I found out his friends nudged Matt along during Purse-gate, I actually loved the story more. His friends didn't control him and make him do anything, but they did show him one little way he could step up. Matt still made the decision to help me and was even willing to walk back to the restaurant with me in the middle of the big game. It was sweet that Matt was willing to jump in but even sweeter that he had friends who wanted to help him be his best. We are made better by good friends. I got Matt at his best that night because he listened to his friends.

Like Matt, I have been on the receiving end of being called up. There was one situation in my life when I was very negative. I was insecure and struggling with gossip about someone. During this time, my best friend Britta graciously said, "I know we both have been in a similar situation as her where we didn't make the best choices, so maybe it isn't our place to talk about her."

Britta was right. It wasn't our place. But the truth is, I was the one talking negatively while Britta gently showed empathy. Still, she didn't act superior to me when she called me up. Britta's tone was kind and graceful to me; it pointed me toward conviction and humility without embarrassing me. I didn't realize how unkind and ungracious I was being until Britta called me up.

In college, there was a point when I was drinking too much. One night, two friends held my hair as I threw up, helped me change my clothes, and got me home safely, and the next day, they had a Gatorade waiting for me. They didn't shame me but first gave me what I needed. Then, after I survived a horrible hangover, they were kind enough to have a hard conversation with me: "Grace, do you think you're walking in God's best? We have been where you are, so please know there's no judgment. You just don't seem yourself or happy."

Friendship can require hard conversations sometimes and just simple nudges at other times.

Friendship can require hard conversations sometimes and just simple nudges at other times. When our friends hurt us or do something we know is not good for them, we want to speak our minds, call them out, and stand our ground. However, that rarely makes anything better. I think our generation has gotten so good at comebacks that we have forgotten how to push our friends to be better in effective and healthy ways. A witty remark may make others laugh or make someone realize they were stupid, but it doesn't always make a friend want to be better. So to clarify, there's an important difference between calling someone up and calling someone out.

Calling someone out. This is typically done in a public setting and involves speaking our minds and aggressively highlighting the friend's wrong deed. It leaves the person feeling shamed, immediately seeing their flaw but not a pathway toward growth. This tactic doesn't show grace, gentleness, and humility.

Calling someone up. When we call someone up, we aren't afraid to humble ourselves to empathize with their mess-up. We don't tell them what they did wrong; we often ask questions or work to help them come to the realization and conviction of what they need to do differently. This tactic sharpens our friends and doesn't belittle them. It listens and cares; it does not judge.

Calling someone up shows love, gentleness, humility, and kindness—all while expressing your love for them and pointing them to God's best. Calling someone out, on the other hand, reveals your own pride. It may tell the truth, but it doesn't show the truth. Yelling at someone to be kinder without using a kind tone can come across as hypocritical. Telling the truth has impact, but showing truth with your words, posture, and grace is transformative.

Let's explore how to make sure our actions call our friends up in helpful, meaningful ways.

7 reminders
about calling friends up, not out

1. Assume the best, and approach gracefully. For example, let's say one of your friends keeps coming home drunk or you've heard they were gossiping about you. Don't immediately assume the worst. We as humans often make mistakes or fall into habits we don't know how to escape. So instead of jumping to conclusions, assume the best and start with prayer. Ask God for the wisdom you need for a graceful conversation.

   A grace-filled approach to a hard conversation can look different for each situation. Sometimes it means admitting you've been in their shoes and have gossiped about others, drunk too much, or forgotten to invite others. At other times, it means asking a simple question first, like, "Are you happy?" A check-in is a great way to approach a conversation and show grace instead of assumptions. Leading with questions gives our friends a chance to share their hearts and present circumstances and brings clarity to the situation. Sincere curiosity shows gentleness and lets their conviction, not our words, lead the conversation.

2. You will never regret encouraging a friend. If someone is struggling with sin, they often need a reminder of their worth rather than a lecture on how they are failing. One time a friend was being short and distant with me. I wanted to get mad and tell her off. However, I prayed for direction and felt like I was supposed to ask her about her anxiety. She had shared with me that her job made her anxious. So I asked how she was doing, and I found out she was struggling with mental health in the midst of a chaotic work month.

    It is sad to think that if I had been quick to get angry, I would have missed a chance to show up for her as a friend. Make sure you show up for your friendship more than you give in to your anger. People often disappoint us when they themselves are disappointed or overwhelmed.

    What my friend needed in that moment wasn't a lecture but a reminder of God's goodness. When we are slow to speak and use gentleness and kindness to first care for our friends, we get closer to the real issue. James 1:19 says, "My dear brothers and sisters, take note of this: Everyone should be quick to listen, slow to speak and slow to become angry." Don't speak your mind; speak the Holy Spirit. The Holy Spirit gives you discernment to approach hard conversations with gentleness, empathy, faithfulness, and goodness.

3. Remember to be willing to be called up too. Oftentimes, it is easier for a friend to receive and listen if they know you,

too, listen regularly to their advice, encouragement, and holy criticism. Honestly, if you and your friends never have conversations about how to grow as humans, disciples, students, and friends, then they may not be friends of goodness. When someone tells you how you can be better, listen. True friendship always involves a posture of humility and vulnerability. None of us are above a healthy conversation leading to growth.

Proverbs 27:17 says, "As iron sharpens iron, so one person sharpens another." Be eager to be sharpened. When someone pushes you to grow, calls you up, reminds you to stop gossiping, or helps you find your purse, trust that their goal is to sharpen you, not to make you feel stupid or to point out your flaws. Their goal is for your good.

Our generation can become easily offended, and when you're easily offended, you're unable to be sharpened. Let your friends make you better, and let your pride take a back seat. Strive to be better, not to prove you're better.

4. Talk to your friend in person. And if that's not an option, use FaceTime. Texting and quick calls lead to confusion. Face-to-face conversation removes confusion and shows how much we care. I think we get so obsessed with being busy that we forget to be clear. Prioritize clarity in all conversations, but especially the ones where you're trying to help and encourage your friends.

I am the person who freaks out when my friend texts, "We need to talk." I can't help but jump to conclusions and wonder, *Does she need to talk about that mistake I made sophomore year in college? Does everyone hate me? Is she mad at me? Did I leave an empty Chick-fil-A cup in her car*

when that's her pet peeve and now our friendship is over?
The friends who truly know me are aware of this anxiety I
get, so instead they will call me, say details about the
topic of the conversation, and reassure me. Do they have
to assure me ahead of time that everything is okay? No,
but they do because they are prioritizing clarity and kindness. Know your friends well enough to also know their
anxious thoughts and more.

5. Give empathy in the conversation. Remember when you've
been in their shoes. I don't think anyone ever grows by
being told "I am better than you." Humility makes friendships feel like a haven, a place of safety. And when you feel
safe, you can grow. Don't seek to prove you're better; seek
to provide a safe space for your friend to see that together
you are both becoming better.

   My hard conversations in friendships drastically im-
proved when I empathized with my friends instead of an-
tagonizing them. If you choose to remove safety, refuge,
and empathy, you are just pointing fingers. Seek to create
haven friendships instead.

6. Keep in mind your friend isn't a villain. The villain is Satan,
who lies to us and deceives us. The problem is the broken-
ness in the world and the insecurity in our minds. Remember that you are on the same team as your friend, and
choose to help them fight off the Enemy together.

   John 10:10 says, "The thief comes only to steal and kill
and destroy. I came that they may have life and have it
abundantly" (ESV). The Enemy wants to steal your peace,
kill your faith, and destroy any relationship that could

make you better. When Jesus is in your heart and life, you have abundant life and abundant friendships. Don't give the Enemy the power to steal the purpose of your conversations.

7. Give your friend space after you talk, but remind them you are there for them. One time, a friend pointed out my habit of complaining about everything. I was being negative, and my friends were annoyed. She talked to me privately, and my first reaction was to say something along the lines of "Are you serious? All I'm doing is venting. Why are you always pushing me down? You complain too."

But before I got the chance for rebuttal, my friend said, "Why don't you take some time to pray about what I said?"

So she gave me time, and I gave myself a chance to catch my breath, receive what she said—and realize that she was right. She was helping me be better. The space my friend gave me allowed me to think about her words and my response. When you trust that you've spoken the truth, give your friend some space to invite God's perspective into the situation. Giving people space to process hard conversations is crucial.

I will be honest: In some friendships, when I tried to have a healthy conversation pushing my friend to be better, it wasn't received well—not because of anything I said or did but because of the other person's ego and conviction. When someone's ego gets pointed out, they don't always take it well. Some people don't know what to do with the feeling of conviction. If you give them space and they push you away, remember that you tried your best to have a holy friendship. Don't give up on them, but don't be insulted because your presence and words made them feel convicted and they didn't receive it.

We're all learning and growing in some way or another. And what our friends don't need is to feel like we're against them. They need to be reminded that we are for them. We show we're trustworthy with their struggles by talking highly about them in rooms they aren't in and respecting them enough to not share their personal stories when it's not appropriate to do so.

Give grace to your friends, keeping in mind that you, too, will have to receive grace from them. Two broken people coming together in friendship means there will be moments of tension, room for improvement, and a need for hard yet holy conversations. Remember, those conversations are for your and your friends' growth, not for awkwardness. Have the hard talks, listen to your friends, and receive their wisdom and words of kindness. Ultimately, the friends who call you up point you to Jesus, the King who sits at the right hand of God the Father. So take a deep breath. God is at work, and the hard conversations will make you both better.

True friendship always involves a posture of humility and vulnerability. None of us are above a healthy conversation leading to growth.

the better friend challenge

- How have you been called out in public? How did that make you feel?

- When have you had someone call you up? How did you receive their words?

- Has ego ever stopped you or someone you know from receiving an important conversation? If so, what happened?

- How can you make your friendships feel like a haven?

truth 7

know the difference between loyal to a fault and loyal to your calling

Something I don't miss about middle school and high school is group projects. I'll never forget when we had a group project in my seventh-grade science class. The popular girl who was on the cheerleading team and hung out with high schoolers sat near me. She asked me if I wanted to be in her group for this project.

Duh! This would mean we would have to hang out after school, and maybe she'd realize she wanted to be actual friends with me, not just science friends. I was so excited that Miss Popular wanted me to be in her group—until it came time to do the project. I kept trying to meet up with Miss Popular, but she was always busy (probably hanging with the high schoolers). I was an over-eager student who didn't like getting bad grades, so this group project became a solo project, and I did it on my own. I was loyal to Miss Popular. She did none of the project and received an A, while I did it all, hoping that somehow she would consider us friends.

However, Miss Popular threw a birthday party about a month later and guess who wasn't invited? Me. I bent over backward to do her work, and she didn't even invite me to her party.

Now, after almost two decades, I am still at times loyal to a fault like I was with Miss Popular. Maybe it didn't look like doing a whole group project, but I have bent over backward for people who didn't truly care about me. And I've learned I'm not the only one who has felt this way. It didn't hit me until I was getting lunch with my friend Victoria and she shared her similar struggle. She told me about some frustrations she was having with people whom she cared about, stuck up for, protected, and tried so hard to grow with. However, she had been let down, left lonely, and pushed aside by the same people she called her best friends.

Similar to Victoria, I have given way more to some friends who didn't seem to care for me well, and it sucked. There are three vivid moments in my friendships that have made me feel loyal to a fault.

In one season, I was always calling one of my best friends first, and we would get on the phone and talk about her love life, her fights with her boyfriend, her job, her sibling's first boyfriend, her outfit, and her. We only talked about her. So I played a little game where I didn't call her back. I waited to see how long it would take her to realize we hadn't talked. We went from talking two times a week to not speaking for two months. Finally, I decided to call her but then wondered, *If I don't mention myself, will we even talk about me at all?* We talked again—but only about her. After that phone call, I realized maybe this wasn't a mutual friendship.

Another time, one of my friends knew I had a big, fat, stupid crush on this freakishly tall guy. I am a firm believer that you can't claim a guy. Life doesn't work that way. Men are not auction items you bid on but potential friendships that could lead somewhere. We were all together at a party, and I noticed my friend—who was single too—flirting with him and putting me down in public, sharing personal stories about me that didn't paint me in a good light. "Grace's closet is always so messy. Have y'all seen it?" she would say with a laugh. I would rather a cute boy not think I was a big slob with a messy closet. Please think of me as wife material in some way. I walked away from that interaction frustrated because she didn't have my back and was belittling me publicly.

The third moment was when a friend wanted to hang out with another of my friends who had a cool job, fancy connections, and more. After I introduced them, I never heard from the first friend again. She got what she wanted, and I was left confused. I would even say she ghosted me. She went from texting and calling me to finding someone more popular and never talking to me again. A lack of mutual care makes a relationship sour.

After I talked to Victoria about our feelings of exhaustion, it got me thinking. *Why am I not praying about my friendships more and asking God for discernment about what friendships to show up for and which ones to let go of?* Both Victoria and I were disappointed by friendships that we viewed in a holy manner. We knew our calling in those friendships was to show our friends Jesus, not to expect Jesus to be shown to us through their actions. I learned how to label the difference: a friendship that is missional versus a friend you're on mission with.

Missional friendships are those friendships of necessity or pleasure where you love radically but trust wisely. Usually in missional friendships, your calling is to pour out, give radical grace and love, and pray for opportunities to show Jesus to them. Even relationships with Christian friends can be missional because these are people you're actively working to support and mentor. It is important to remember they are people, not projects. But in these friendships, you should expect little and give a lot. This type of relationship might feel one-sided, but you have a sense and calling that God has brought these people into your life for a special reason or a particular season. You love them well—not because they can give you anything in return but because Christ radically loves them.

> *You love them well—not because they can give you anything in return but because Christ radically loves them.*

In a missional friendship, you might want to keep some things private. And you may have to be extra aware of the setting of the hangout. You may have to choose a time and location that will help you stay focused on giving energy and care to your friend.

Also, understand the difference between privacy and secrecy. Secrets are not holy to have, but privacy is a healthy discernment tool used to protect yourself from people whom it isn't wise to trust. A secret is when we purposefully keep something just to ourselves because we feel shame, embarrassment, fear, or pride about it. Keeping something private is when we choose to be careful about sharing our vulnerabilities, our struggles, our hardships, and even some celebrations with only trusted friends. These trusting, safe friendships teach us humility, empathy, kindness, and radical grace.

In contrast to missional relationships, friends you're on mission with are those who run the good race alongside you. They aren't perfect, but they seek to love you and see you, and you love and see them. The goal of these friendships is to become better together. They involve trust. That doesn't mean you share all private matters equally with every holy friend; some may be closer than others and can know more private, intimate matters. But there is always a level of holy trust in these friendships. These friends show clarity, and they pour into you, just as you pour into them. You love each other well, and your friendship consistently reflects God's love. The connection isn't about their status, wealth, or popularity. It is about your same God, your same purpose, and shared interests. It's about a deep desire to see each other—flaws and all—and make each other better. Conflicts will arise, but you are both still invested. You don't expect perfection from these friends, but you can and should expect genuine care, just as you should also care for them consistently and regularly.

No friendship is a perfect fifty-fifty where you each give and receive equal amounts. Both of you will fall, and sometimes you'll be in a season where you can give only twenty or your friend can give only thirty. Still, each of you works hard to be there for the other and stay loyal to your calling.

Being loyal to a fault happens when you expect missional friends to act like co-mission friends. Disappointment happens when you trust people who don't care for you in a way that reflects God's love. When we put ourselves out there and seek friends to be on mission with, we may still end up occasionally feeling disappointed and lonely. But if we commit to being loyal to the Author of love and the close friends He's given us, it is never "to a fault"; it is always to His glory.

Being loyal to a fault happens when you expect missional friends to act like co-mission friends.

One woman I love in the Bible is Ruth. I think she showed loyalty well. Ruth had every excuse to be selfish because life did not go her way at first. She lost her husband, her father-in-law, and her brother-in-law. Because of the culture she lived in, we can assume that as a childless widow, she was at risk of being poor and taken advantage of. Her mother-in-law advised her to go back to her mother's house and do what was best for herself, but Ruth said this to her: "Where you go I will go, and where you lodge I will lodge. Your people shall be my people, and your God my God. Where you die I will die, and there will I be buried."[1]

Ruth cared about loving Naomi more than doing what was "normal." While she had every right to be selfish, she chose to be loyal to Naomi and their God-given friendship. That's what you do when you care for someone well. It isn't about what you get from the world but about the fellowship that comes from walking through life together, including the good and the bad. Some may say Ruth was loyal to a fault because she risked her own comfort. But as we look back on this story thousands of years later, we see the full picture: Ruth's loyalty was loving. She showed God's love, and her loyalty led her to future blessings. It led her to a man named Boaz, who loved her, cared for her, and protected both her and Naomi. Was she loyal just so she would receive blessings? No, but God loves to lead His obedient, faithful children to His best.

My best friend Anna and I have been friends since we were nineteen years old. We have seen each other through lows and highs. She sent me cookies when a boy broke my heart, and I remember her telling me about her and her husband's first kiss. At one point her dad got sick and passed away. Even as an author, in situations like that, I never know what to say. I felt awful, but I knew my words would never be enough. When I called my dad to tell him about her dad dying, he simply said, "You need to show up to the funeral."

I was confused by his advice. I lived two and a half hours away, and I didn't really know her dad. I didn't want to bother her by showing up. My dad was stern and continued, "You don't need to tell her what you're going to do. Just do it."

I did. I showed up at a funeral home cities away. When she saw me, she was shocked. I don't do a lot of things right, but listening to my dad in that moment was the right choice. I may not have known her dad, but I knew Anna, who loved her dad.

Anna later told me that she had been upset because I hadn't said anything to comfort her about her dad's passing. She didn't know I was stressed about what to say. But when I showed up, it was exactly what she needed. She was going through one of the toughest experiences of her life, and she wanted to know people in her life cared for her and would be there.

Be unreasonably loyal to the friends you're on mission with. We may not always have the perfect words, but we do have the ability to show up. You will never regret physically showing up for a friend. And don't feel pathetic when you are kind and show up for people who wouldn't necessarily show up for you. I hope you remember that loyalty and trust are gifts for those closest to you but going out of your way to be kind to others and show up for them, regardless of whether they're there for you, is a way to honor God and celebrate Christ in you. Extend your loyalty to your cherished friends, but know that kindness and love is a gift as a Christian you should share with all.

*Loyalty shows up. Loyal friends show up to celebrate,
to mourn, and to be there for you.*

7 truths
about loyalty

When I was younger, my friendships were shallow because I was seeking to have fun, not to be loyal. Fun was great for a bit, but I would get distracted and not do the more important things. Fun won't be there for you when your boyfriend decides to leave on a random Tuesday. Fun won't talk through your job offers and give you wisdom. Fun won't stay by your side even when others in your friend group gossip about you. Fun won't care for you and help you if your divorce means moving out in the middle of heartbreak.

Loyalty is love in action. It is one of the most important characteristics we have in best friends. If you want to show loyalty in friendships, remember these seven truths.

1. Loyalty shows up. Loyal friends show up to celebrate, to mourn, and to be there for you. Whether it's to give you a ride from the airport, support you at a funeral, throw a housewarming party or baby shower for you, celebrate your promotion, or just cry with you when life doesn't go how you planned, you never have to beg a loyal friend to show up.

2. Loyalty is honest, even when it is hard. It tells the truth with courage and mercy, grace and gentleness, yet clearly

shows you how you can be better. A shallow friend may lie to you and make you believe you don't need to change. A loyal friend isn't afraid to call you higher and lead you to better.

3. Loyalty leads you to peace. It reminds you that even in the midst of rejection, chaos, rumors, and loneliness, someone is always in your corner. Loyalty reassures you that you are valued, loved, appreciated, and cherished despite the outside voices and pressures of life that seem to speak otherwise. When you remember the people who are in your corner, you have peace even if you're surrounded by others seeking to bring you down.

4. Loyalty is consistent. It doesn't waver or make you guess; it stays the same. A truly loyal friend isn't faithful to you only when they feel like it, when they're rewarding you for doing something they wanted, or when it's easy and convenient. They're just as caring on your good days as on your bad days.

5. Loyalty will always protect your name in rooms you're not in. Loyal friends stand firm in their love for you and don't waver even if others are talking about you. They don't publicly critique or humiliate you to make themselves look better.

6. Loyalty involves a mutual care for each other; it is shared between two trusting, close friends. It gives and receives. You can't receive loyalty in a holy manner without also giving it in return. Will you always have the energy and

love to give others care and consideration? Probably not. Both you and your friends will have hardships that make it difficult for you to show up for one another. Loyalty, though, is about knowing there is consistent, mutual care, even during hard seasons. Give grace regularly, but expect loyalty consistently.

7. Loyalty is a picture of Christ. Christ was and is loyal to us, consistently showing up and loving us. Romans 8:37–39 says, "In all these things we are more than conquerors through him who loved us. For I am convinced that neither death nor life, neither angels nor demons, neither the present nor the future, nor any powers, neither height nor depth, nor anything else in all creation, will be able to separate us from the love of God that is in Christ Jesus our Lord." Obviously, Christ's love is more loyal and loving than any earthly friendship. Yet I do believe He gives us holy, vibrant earthly friendships that can reflect His love if we make Him the foundation. If our friendships reflect His love, then maybe they should reflect His loyalty too.

May God protect our friendships from fights over silly boys who need haircuts and from our insecurities when we feel like our friends aren't reaching out enough. May God protect us from the Enemy trying to separate us from good community. May nothing separate us from the beautiful friendships God has given us.

May nothing separate us from the beautiful
friendships God has given us.

the better friend challenge

- When have you felt loyal to a fault? What was your response, and why?

- Who in your life has earned your trust enough to hear your private confessions and struggles?

- Have you ever trusted a missional friend too much and become disappointed or hurt?

- Identify the current people in your life who are missional friends versus friends you're on mission with.

- How can you be radically loyal—not to a fault but for a purpose?

truth 8

beware of your mess, and show grace

I've lived with many girls around my age, and most of the time it was in a crusty house. Living with other girls can be a fun, fruitful adventure of killing spiders, watching *Love Is Blind*, and cooking fresh shrimp tacos together. There is always the giggling before a first date, borrowing clothes before any kind of fun social function, and small passive-aggressive placement of one person's shoes by their door because the other person hates shoes in the living room. (Sorry, roommates!)

I chose to have roommates because I knew I needed community. Is living with other single girls sometimes hard? Yes. I had some roommates who were my best friends and others who were not my friends. But did living with them make me better? I'd like to think so.

Here's some things that always happened when I lived with other girls:

We always said we needed to "have a roomie dinner soon" and we meant it . . . sometimes.

We screen-shared texts and overanalyzed interactions with boys. Was this healthy? Maybe not. But it was part of the regular routine.

Someone always forgot to lock the door, and then there would be a text reminder in the group message.

We would say, "Let's have a movie night," and then spend two hours looking through our streaming services for a movie none of us had watched or all of us would be down for. By the time we found one, it would be late, and no matter what, one roommate would fall asleep during the movie. (Yes, I'm talking about you, Ramsey.)

Someone would open the fridge and yell, "Ew, who left this?" while holding up some weird rotten vegetable. When grocery shopping, we always got vegetables but often forgot (or chose to forget) they were options for us to eat. Suddenly our fresh leafy greens were limp, moldy, and rotten, causing the whole refrigerator to stink and need to be cleaned as soon as possible.

Sometimes we would put off the important but gross fridge cleaning. Other times, after one whiff, we would all realize it had to be done right then. I used to joke that fridge cleaning was the most vulnerable part of living together. We would line up in our kitchen, and one person would be in charge of searching the refrigerator for old expiration dates, Tupperware of rotten leftovers, and rotten vegetables. A second person would hold a trash bag, and the third person would have the cleaning spray, paper towels, and dishwasher ready.

One time my favorite roommates, Maile and Ramsey, and I did the dreaded fridge cleaning together. We spent three hours on a Saturday afternoon yelling "Ew!" and "Who did this?" Maile had left a weird salad dressing she made from scratch sit too long in a Tupperware container, and Ramsey would keep even one-fifth of a leftover avocado wrapped in the refrigerator and never end up using it. I was probably the girl who had left the moldy vegetables that caused the whole fridge cleaning to begin with. We laughed and screamed at the weird dripping liquids while rushing them to the trash bag, and suddenly, after we came together, the fridge was better.

One time a cute boy came over before the dreaded fridge cleaning and asked, "Who left this?" We girls laughed and just looked at each other, silently agreeing that we would not tell him. He didn't need to know whose fault it was. We needed to do the cleaning together. I will confess: The gross stuff was mine. But I am thankful for friends who focused on keeping my confessions and mess private.

Maile, Ramsey, and I did many fun things together. We went to Universal Orlando, the beach, and the mountains and on many adventures together. But still, those fridge cleanings were some of my favorites. Even something as annoying as cleaning could feel purposeful and fun when we worked together, gave grace for all our mess-ups, and focused on the task at hand: making our world a little better.

Not all my friendships have been like my relationship with Maile and Ramsey. Some past friends and I have chosen to be passive-aggressive, hide our struggle, and shy away from hard conversations. We have avoided our "cleaning out the fridge" moments and, in return, missed out on deepening and better-ing our friendship.

I remember finding out that a different roommate in another situation had talked about me behind my back, saying I was frustrating her and she didn't enjoy living with me. She also shared a personal struggle I was working through with strangers at a party in a different state. This surprised me because I had assumed my roommate and I were friends, and I thought friends didn't talk about each other, especially when they weren't in the same room. Another friend overheard her and warned me not to keep sharing my junk with this "friend." After I heard this, I confronted her. She apologized and didn't deny it, which I appreciated and admired. She confessed that she said it out of sin. We moved on because that is life, but I learned to not share the messy fridge of my heart with her.

True friends clean the fridge together, but if outside forces ask about the mess, they don't point fingers; they switch the conversation. Holy loyalty focuses on making you better in private and always respecting your name, even in rooms you aren't in.

Good friends care about your mess and work on their own messes too. They don't let you sit there and rot while your mess becomes worse.

Good friends care about your mess and work on their own messes too. They don't let you sit there and rot while your mess becomes worse. We all have at one point left our shoes on the floor, kept our leftovers in the refrigerator too long, or forgotten to lock the door or ask permission to borrow a sweater. If you allow your mess to stay too long in a friendship, it gets rotten, smells, and causes the whole friendship to suffer. But when you work together to refine your character and clean out your sins, insecurity, and doubt, you find goodness.

We have become so used to our junk that we aren't startled by it, but when we see other people's junk, we are annoyed, impatient, and frustrated.

I think it's easy to be aware of other people's mess-ups while unaware of our own. We have become so used to our junk that we aren't startled by it, but when we see other people's junk, we are annoyed, impatient, and frustrated. I was not aware of leaving my shoes in the living room, but I was aware of my roommate leaving the lights on. Instead of being annoyed by others' junk, we need to strive to be aware of our own and work toward having a friendship that seeks to grow together.

Matthew 7:3–5 says, "Why do you look at the speck of sawdust in your brother's eye and pay no attention to the plank in your own eye? How can you say to your brother, 'Let me take the speck out of your eye,' when all the time there is a plank in your own eye? You hypocrite, first take the plank out of your own eye, and then you will see clearly to remove the speck from your brother's eye."

I am often reminded of the importance of this when dealing with friends, roommates, community, family, and others. In this broken world, you will befriend someone who occasionally has a speck in their eye. It is good for you to point out their speck—their gossip, their sin, and their hiccups—but make sure *you* are eager and willing to consistently work on living a life that reflects God's goodness.

In fact, I would even say true and good friendships regularly have "let's clean out our fridge together" moments where you refine each other. Psalm 133:1 says, "How good and pleasant it is when God's people live together in unity!" Living in unity doesn't mean you just watch your favorite show together. Unity can actually look like this:

- A time of confession, where you come together and release whatever sin you're struggling with. This means being honest about the sin that feels like it's been rotting in your heart for too long.

- A time of accountability and encouragement, where you simply remind your friend of their worth and the blessings that come from choosing obedience. Unity is pleasant, even when life isn't. A united friendship is deeply united to God, pointing each person to the Savior and Creator.

- An honest check-in, asking how a friend is doing around a holiday when she is still grieving someone who left too soon.

- A dinner conversation where you help your friend process a choice about what job to take or city to move to. Being united doesn't mean you will always be in the same physical place or even share the same opinion. It means inviting one another into your decisions so you can pray for each other and hear sound wisdom from God.

These moments of unity don't have to be miserable and sad and hard. Just like Maile, Ramsey, and I shared bonding moments over cleaning out our messes, you can enjoy the sweet and laughter-filled moments of accountability, confession, and honest check-ins. Moments like this can take place in the privacy of your home, at the park on a sunny day, on a walk after work, while eating sushi and drinking red wine, or even on a phone call stretching miles across the country. Friendship isn't *only* about having fun together; it's about growing together. When you become better together, you have true community.

Give grace to your friend for their mess because you have a mess of your own. Be self-aware, let grace lead your actions and your words, and push each other to be better. And make sure your friend can trust you with how you care for and protect their name in private and in public. Their mess isn't for the world to know; it is for you and them to be aware of so you can help your friend be better.

Friends who do life together have the opportunity to make one another either better and holier or worse and more distracted from their purpose. One group of friends I had in Orlando became really good at asking questions. We created a dinner club where we met at restaurants we loved or hadn't tried yet. We wore cute clothes, ordered cute cocktails, and talked about life. Yet slowly we realized our conversations had changed from life things to negative thoughts, negative energy, and gossip. It became a time where we didn't make each other better anymore.

I remember leaving one of those dinners feeling like a worse version of myself. I loved hanging out with them, so it wasn't their fault, but together we weren't using our time wisely. In our busy schedules, we didn't have time to necessarily talk every day. We needed to have conversations during the dinner club that were more intentional than our random discussions of pop culture, reality shows, and our high school bullies.

Annie, one of the dinner-club members, was always so good about checking in with the rest of us. At the start of one dinner, I remember her saying, "Let's ask each other more questions about ourselves!" Annie led us to unity in that moment. Together, we made the choice to have conversations that were caring to both one another and our God.

So, without hesitation, we started asking more and deeper questions, and we watched our friendship transform from girls getting to know one another to girls making one another better. I began to leave the dinner clubs feeling better instead of worse. I went from being in company with these friends to being challenged by them to become a better version of myself. I saw their messes, flaws, hurts, and doubt. We switched careers, got into relationships, and fumbled through life together. But each time we would sit at dinner club, we would ask questions that caused us to reflect, recount, rally, or race. Good questions to ask friends often fall into one of these four R's.

Reflect. Friends ask questions that lead you to reflect. It can be about a big test you just took or the conversation with your boss about the raise you wanted. Reflection questions ask not what happened but how: How did it go? How did you feel before, during, and after? How did you react? They allow you to reflect on your mental, spiritual, and physical health during the events that happened. True friends show interest and allow one another time to process their thoughts and feelings.

Recount. As friends, we need to confess and recount moments during our private and public lives where we have fallen short. We normally want to move on and find "friends" who will make us forget about our sin and shortcomings, but that doesn't make us better. When we recount, we need trusted friends who will empathize and hear our sins with kindness and gentleness but push us to God's grace and an obedient life of surrender to Him. Make sure you find friends who ask you about your sin and listen while pushing you to the cross. Don't entertain friends who laugh about their sin. Our sin breaks God's heart. So when your friends laugh about that guy you hooked up with, the gossip you shared, the mean comment you made to the annoying girl, or any of your sin, they are laughing at something God weeps at. Proverbs 14:9 says, "Fools mock at making amends for sin, but goodwill is found among the upright." Don't become a friend group who laughs and mocks at sin. Instead, seek to live a holy life and make amends, and in return God will lead you to goodwill.

Rally. When I had my first book-release party, my best friend Britta was living in California. She simply asked me the date of my party and then traveled on two horribly long Spirit flights to Orlando to attend the party and rally behind me. I will never forget that. She asked one question— "When?"—and showed up for me. Rallying can simply be cheering your friends on and helping them feel hyped up, celebrated, or appreciated. Sometimes a friend needs you to rally behind them when they are going through a hard, difficult, hurtful, or confusing season. As friends, we are called to rally for each other and champion our friends. One time at the dinner club, Karly shared she was leaving her nanny job and was considering other careers. Together we rallied behind her, encouraged her, and spoke into the giftings we saw in her. To rally, ask questions that show celebration, hope, and interest during the good seasons and ones that show care, empathy, and interest during hard seasons. Romans 12:15 says, "Rejoice with those who rejoice, weep with those who weep" (ESV). When you rally behind those you love, you rejoice when they rejoice and you weep when they weep. Keep in mind, sometimes it's not about asking for more details. Once, a friend went through a breakup, and I stupidly asked, "Do you think he was lying?" when all she wanted to do was mourn and not overthink. A better question in that moment would have been "Do you know you're worth more than that?" or even "Do you want to talk about it more or maybe not talk about it over ice cream?"

Race. Friends ask questions that help you race toward the ultimate goal: Jesus Christ. I have had some friendships where it felt like we were racing toward the wrong goals, like significant others, success, popularity, or gossip. But when you both race after Jesus, you are walking toward God's best. Make sure your questions help each other do that; there is no greater joy than experiencing God's best alongside your sisters in Christ. Racing is different from the other R's because it reminds you and your friends of where you're going. When you reflect, recount, and rally, you help someone remember and share what has happened and encourage them in their present circumstances. But when you race, you push your friends to the ultimate goal. Hebrews 12:1–2 says, "Since we are surrounded by such a great cloud of witnesses, let us throw off everything that hinders and the sin that so easily entangles. And let us run with perseverance the race marked out for us, fixing our eyes on Jesus, the pioneer and perfecter of faith." After you throw off what entangles you by recounting, you are ready to race, and the best part is that when you find holy and good friendships, your friends race toward Jesus with you.

So, if a friendship feels shallow, don't settle for it. It is up to you to initiate deeper questions that lead to a deeper understanding of each other.

So, if a friendship feels shallow, don't settle for it. It is up to you to initiate deeper questions that lead to a deeper understanding of each other. Surely God can transform your friendships into those of cheering one another on and becoming better together.

7 questions
to ask your friends regularly

1. How has this week challenged you? What worry has consumed your thoughts lately?

2. What is something in your life that is causing you to overthink? Is there anything you need prayer for?

3. When was a time you felt more celebrated by your friendships? How can I celebrate you better?

4. What music, podcasts, shows, or advice are you currently listening to or watching? Are these resources helping you or hindering your growth?

5. When have you felt lonely or overlooked by those in your life, including me?

6. What do you think is currently a distraction in my life? Are you concerned about any areas or habits in my life that seem to be distracting me from my purpose?

7. When you think of your future, are you excited, nervous, or anxious? Where do you see yourself?

the better friend challenge

- What would you say is the current mess you're working through?

- How can you recognize your mess, be aware of your friends' messes, and work together to be better?

- What do accountability and confession look like in the middle of a crazy week?

- How can you protect your friends' names in rooms they aren't in?

truth 9

friendship breakups are hard
but can still be holy

I remember being seventeen years old and crying over a guy who broke my heart. He left me confused and hurt when he dumped me for another girl. I stared at my spinning ceiling fan at about 1:30 A.M., with an empty pit in my stomach, wondering what went wrong. I replayed the conversations we had. *Was I too much? Not enough? Did I bother him when I asked him to show up a little more? Maybe he didn't think I was fun enough, or honestly maybe I wasn't good at making him happy.*

I cried. I overthought our whole relationship. I ate a pint of Ben and Jerry's ice cream one day and then the next day couldn't stomach the thought of food. I even posted bikini pictures thinking that would make him miss me. It did get me texts from his friends, but not him. He didn't care. He was with another girl, not caring about me.

I knew it was time for me to move on.

Ten years later, I was in a popping, shiny city for a meeting with my publisher. I didn't realize it was his town now. I got a text from him, the same guy who broke my heart as a teenage girl. I was worried about a big meeting and working on a few projects—then his name flashed on my phone, and suddenly I was seventeen again.

"Hey, Grace! This might sound weird, but I saw you were in Nashville, and I would love to catch up and get a drink."

Catch up? Was that code for he wanted me back? *The cool high school jock realizes he missed out on me and wants another chance.*

I looked at my suitcase packed with professional clothes and knew that none of them would do. I had to go shopping for a cuter outfit that screamed, *I'll make you regret leaving me for the dance-team girl,* and I had to prepare for showing him that he missed out.

After buying not just a new outfit but even fresh mascara, I got ready to see the boy who could've been mine. He picked me up at my hotel and bought me a drink, and we sat together after a decade of not talking and caught up. And guess what happened? There were sparks and butterflies, and we lived happily ever after. *Kidding, of course.* In reality, nothing happened. We talked, and my outfit looked good. But as I sat there, laughing at myself acting like a teenage girl, I realized maybe God knew what He was doing. The guy was more mature, and so was I. But sitting in a booth at a poorly lit bar with random country music playing, I realized that the breakup that once broke me was a good thing.

My favorite thing about God is that a bad thing can become a good thing if you make it a God thing. The breakup that had caused me anguish and tears turned out to be the best thing that happened to me. He was a great guy now, but as I stared at him all these years later, I realized both of us were our best selves because we weren't together. We weren't meant to be a couple. A random meetup with an ex-boyfriend showed me that I just needed perspective. What had hurt me so badly ten years before was actually a blessing.

I've had difficult breakups, crying over guys I dated and guys I didn't even date, but I have also felt a similar, if not worse, pain over girl friendships that ended. Friendship breakups are hard. Just like with boy-girl breakups, they cause a sinking feeling in the pit of my stomach, make me freak out if the ex-friend texts after disappearing for a while, and lead me to overthink what all went wrong. But there aren't many Taylor Swift songs for you when you go through friend breakups.

I had a friend betray me so badly it hurt and caused distrust in future friendships.

I had a friend ghost me and go from wanting to be my friend to not texting back.

I had a friend who moved away and didn't even try to stay connected.

Then there was the day that one of my closest friends and I realized our friendship caused more stress than blessings, so we both decided to walk away.

Some of these friend breakups ended in fights, insults, gossip, and betrayal. Others ended with confusion, ghosting, and no words. But the healthiest friend breakup I experienced was the one that ended with a conversation and a calm, mutual decision to walk away. We disagreed, and that was okay. Was there still a sinking feeling and a sadness that felt like grief? Of course. But there was also peace in realizing that I was walking away from something that wasn't for me.

That's the beauty of friend breakups. They can be hard and uncomfortable, but they can also be holy because they aren't about you walking away from something; they are about you walking toward God's best.

My teenage heartbreak was good. Was it hard on me? Yes. Ten years later, I didn't need a meetup with the guy who wasn't meant for me. I needed a reminder that the breakup was about what God had in store for me, not about what wasn't for me.

My friend breakups were also blessings. The friend who betrayed me taught me the importance of seeking friends I could trust and of prioritizing wisdom over coolness and kindness over being similar. The breakup was hard. Yet through it I learned that we can't control how people treat us but we can control whether we trust them again. Proverbs 26:11 says, "As a dog returns to its vomit, so fools repeat their folly." The Bible calls you a fool if you return to your bad habits, sin, and even the people who repeatedly lead you to hurt, confusion, and pain.

It is also important to note that Jesus knows what it's like to be betrayed. Although you shouldn't trust a hurtful friend so readily, you should love radically like Jesus. Jesus knew Judas would betray Him, and His response was to wash his feet and feed him dinner.[1] It wasn't to speak His mind, cause a scene, and freak out. He radically loved and cared for His betrayer. You don't need to trust friends who hurt you again, and you might need to walk away, but always end it with love.

The friend who ghosted me taught me that I am worth more than confusion. Overthinking what went wrong does no good, and I had to accept that I probably enjoyed that friend's potential more than their kindness. A kind friend wouldn't ghost me on a random Tuesday. I don't need to be friends with anyone who doesn't want to be friends with me. Friendship should bring joy, not overthinking, consistent anxiety, and stress.

The mutual friendship breakup taught me that sometimes, no matter how hard you try, God may not have destined you to do life together. I tried so hard for a friendship that just exhausted me. It didn't mean either one of us was a villain; it just meant God had better plans. In Acts 15:36–41, Paul and Barnabas were building up the early church and had a disagreement. These friends had been doing life together but disagreed about what to do next in their ministry. So they argued and parted ways. Now, here we are, two thousand years later, and we know that the church grew because of the faithfulness of both Barnabas and Paul. There was no villain in this story, and their parting actually led them both to go where God called.

The mutual friendship breakup taught me that sometimes, no matter how hard you try, God may not have destined you to do life together.

You're allowed to have sharp disagreements. You're allowed to have different opinions and preferences and still be friends.

Sometimes the holiest thing you can do is walk away.

It is hard to discern when it is time to forgive, agree, and make up and when it is time to walk away. You will never be able to discern this unless you pray. Instead of just talking to God about the friendship, ask Him whether this friendship is in His will. Pray for both your mission and your friend, and give the friendship to God. Often the most powerful prayer is as simple as *Lord, have Your way.* It feels scary to lose control over our friendships. But if we trust that the God who created our hearts will lead us to community, we will be led to people who make us better and reflect His glory in this world. Let the Lord have His way in your friendships. Pray for the friendship, pray for discernment, and seek clarity about whether a friendship needs to end.

If we do discern that a friendship should end, it is hard to know how to do that. I mean, in romantic relationships, most everyone agrees that a clear breakup with words is needed before the two people move on. Yet there is no universally accepted way to end a friendship. If you feel it is time to end a friendship, here are a few simple guidelines:

1. How you approach the breakup depends on how close the friendship was. Is this just an old college friend you've lost touch with? Or is this a former bridesmaid who treated you in an unkind way? The depth of the friendship reflects the depth and care needed for the breakup.

2. Choose clarity always. Sometimes there is no need for a conversation; the end of the friendship is clear enough because of time, an event, or a lack of presence in each other's lives. However, you will never regret choosing clarity. Clarity leads to peace.

3. If they don't want to have a conversation, you can't force them. Be kind enough to yourself to not beg for respect from someone who doesn't care about you. On the other hand, you're allowed to choose peace over a long, drawn-out conversation. After praying, if you know a conversation will only add disorder and slow your healing, simply say one time, "This friendship no longer suits me. I hope the best for you," and move on. You don't need to reply anymore, and you can walk away trusting that God gave you discernment and will also give them what they need.

4. If there is a conversation, always apologize for what you could've done better. Even if the friendship's end seems like fully their fault, pray for humility so God may reveal something you need to apologize for. We can always acknowledge that we can be better.

5. Thank them. You may have the opportunity to thank them personally, or you may only get to internally thank them because you can't have or don't want a conversation. Even if they hurt you, even if they were only in your life for a short time, they made you better because God is powerful enough to make a bad thing a good thing. All the people you meet can make you better if you thank God for His ability to use even their presence to refine you.

6. Remember that gentleness and self-control show Christ's love. Be gentle with your ex-friends. Be kind to them and their names. Not everyone needs to know what happened. Trust that God is working for your good and that the truth will always manifest. You will never regret walking away with gentleness and trusting God to let the truth be revealed in His perfect will.

7. Seek to learn what explains their behavior. That doesn't mean the explanation excuses their behavior. But learning why someone does something can help you empathize with them.

after the breakup

Bitterness is an ugly feeling. Sometimes the friendship breakup isn't your choice. It may have even been created because of human sin, so not only are you bitter, but you're also hurt. When the story of your life doesn't go your way, you have two options: You can let it expand your heart with hope for better or you can let it create a bitter heart. Don't allow the devil to use your friendship breakups to stop you from having hope in God for something new. For the longest time, I let bad friendships stop me from living in the hope of God's ability to bring new blessings. I would transfer my trust issues onto new, pure friendships because my heart was bitter.

When the story of your life doesn't go your way, you have two options: You can let it expand your heart with hope for better or create a bitter heart.

A bitter heart believes that everyone will hurt and leave you eventually. A bitter heart can't look beyond past hurts and doesn't remember the goodness of God to make a way.

A hopeful heart trusts God to lead you to new blessings. It still has wisdom, but it doesn't plan for the worst possible outcome to happen. It hopes with a willing spirit for God to guide you to what is good, true, and beautiful.

We must fight bitterness in our hearts. On the days you struggle to trust God's ability to do something new and bring you His joy after past hurts, remember this:

> Create in me a pure heart, O God,
>   and renew a steadfast spirit within me.
> Do not cast me from your presence
>   or take your Holy Spirit from me.
> Restore to me the joy of your salvation
>   and grant me a willing spirit, to sustain me.
>   —Psalm 51:10–12

This psalm is an honest prayer you can use to cry out to God when you experience bitterness. Yes, you've been hurt, but you can't allow your hurt to create a bitter heart that removes joy and takes you farther from the Holy Spirit. Allow God to make that psalm come alive in you:

- to create in you a pure heart in place of a bitter heart
- to keep you in His presence and not in your hurt
- to restore the joy that comes from your salvation, not from life going your way
- to give you a willing spirit to sustain you, enabling you to see the blessings coming your way and His presence at work in your life

---

Hope is more powerful than bitterness.

Hope is more powerful than bitterness. Hope comes from the Lord's goodness; therefore, it is a powerful force from God that never ends, doesn't give up, and shows you God's glory—even when you're faced with sorrow. Yes, you've been hurt, but you have a Savior ready and willing to give healing. God is more powerful than any pain, and He provides clarity in our confusing world. Ask for a spirit willing to try again.

When we look back on our friendship breakups, we might see betrayal, confusion, or sharp disagreement—but I pray we always see God's faithfulness too. It is not our job to understand what exactly went wrong. It is our job to realize that if the door is closed, God is leading us to better. When I think of my most painful friend breakups, I see hurt, but I also see the friendships that were waiting on the other side of those closed doors. May you trust that the hardest friendship breakup of your life is actually a holy rerouting to what's meant for you.

God is more powerful than any pain, and He provides clarity in our confusing world.

7 signs
it's time to end a friendship

"So, how have you been?" a friend asked me during our lunch date.

This was another forced, awkward hangout with someone who had once been a best friend. We found each other in our party phase, and we both cleaned up our acts and worked at becoming better together. She was a lifeline for me during that season, and we leaned on each other. But something had changed. We had a few disagreements. Sometimes we hung out too much, and one person wouldn't get the other's sarcasm. Miscommunication would happen. One of us was friends with the new girlfriend of the other's ex-boyfriend. One person hosted a group dinner and forgot to invite the other. A couple of awkward hangouts later, we sat in silence.

After the latest strained lunch date, I called my friend and shared with her my consistent hurt in this friendship, the confusion I always felt about whether she liked me, and my feelings about all our disagreements. I finally honestly said what I had been thinking for a while: "I always leave our interactions feeling hurt and confused, and our friendship is exhausting me." We had a candid conversation, and she shared hurts she experienced from me. Maybe we were both misunderstanding each other, but neither of us was happy or finding fulfillment in this friendship. Both of us were frustrated, and our communication was incompatible. I used to think it was because she was wrong and awful and gave up on me. But once I looked at our friendship honestly, I realized that neither of us did anything wrong. We just weren't meant to be friends.

After that phone call, we went our separate ways. I later saw a picture of her baby, a beautiful girl with a cute lavender bow. When I saw her precious daughter, I smiled. I wasn't sad that I wouldn't know her little girl; I was thankful that I met this friend right when we needed each other.

Some people are friends for a lifetime; others, just for a season. This relationship made me better, but then we outgrew each other. We didn't click anymore, and that's okay. You don't need to force a friendship that no longer fits—just like I didn't need to force myself into a dress that was one size too small to wear to a party. Yes, I was able to get into it and make it fit, but it was uncomfortable. Discomfort is a sign that things aren't the way they were made to be.

I once got an invitation to the wedding of a former best friend. We never had a conversation to end our friendship. Honestly, we just went our separate ways. I fought for the friendship more, and she only talked to me when she and her boyfriend fought. I felt hurt that she didn't respond to me and seemed to give up on me. When she invited me to her wedding, for the first time I knew where we stood. As I held the invitation, I knew it wasn't my place to go. I finally found peace in realizing we were no longer friends.

Finding the peace and awareness of a friendship ending is important. Peace is a person: Jesus Christ. So it isn't so much about finding a feeling but about finding God's goodness in a hard goodbye.

Reflect on these seven reminders so you can see whether it is time to end a friendship:

1. Friendship will always be work, but it shouldn't be constantly uncomfortable and stressful. Does meeting up or calling each other bring stress and not joy, peace, or goodness? Then it may be time to walk away. Friendship is something you have to fight for, but there should be signs that the other person is fighting for it too. If you're the only one fighting to stay connected, then you're exhausting yourself. Friendship is a mutual choice. If both people aren't trying, then you might need to accept the other person's subtle choice.

2. If the only thing that brought you together was a singular experience or place, then it might be time to walk away. If you have nothing else in common anymore, that's okay. The friendship may have been only for a season and not one God has for your future. On the other hand, it could be that this season just looks different for this friendship and it's not over forever. Even though you may not talk often, maybe the friendship is low-maintenance right now and meant to be a relationship you catch up with occasionally—and perhaps will prove invaluable to both of you years later when life looks different. Ask God for discernment to know the difference.

3. Friendship should bring you laughter, not a consistent fear that your friend is laughing at you. You don't need to be around anyone who mocks you, a child of God.

4. If you don't trust them, you may need to walk away. Friendship builds trust and confidence, not suspicion. If you worry about how the person talks about you in rooms you're not in, then they aren't a friend. Trust your girl gut and walk away.

5. If certain friends aren't gently challenging you, you may need to distance yourself from them. I call these "yes friends." They always agree with you and never question you, even when a situation or a decision is obviously not good for you. Good friends ask good questions, offer gentle correction when needed, and are honest enough to disagree with you. If your friends are recklessly giving you poor advice, they are recklessly leading you away from Christ.

6. Friends should celebrate whatever season you're in. When I was the only single friend, one girl acted better than me because she was in a relationship. Another friend reminded me of God's perfect timeline for my life. The friend who dragged me down and made me doubt God's goodness because of my relationship status was one I had to walk away from. The friends you should stay close to are the ones who encourage you with God's timeline and don't act better than you but make you better.

7. When you feel peace that God has done all He meant to do in a friendship, it may be time to part ways with that

friend. This doesn't mean you won't mourn and become sad. Peace and sadness can exist at the same time. But when you feel peace that a friendship is over and that there's nothing left to do, trust that. Mourn the loss, yet expect God to lead you to your purpose and peace in the sadness.

When we look back on our friendship breakups—friends who ghosted us, confused us, or betrayed us or friends we just outgrew—we can become sad, or we can trust that God has done all He intended to do. God's timing is perfect. Be thankful for His timing and for His using the friendship to make you better, even if it was painful and hard. The one who gossiped about you taught you the power of words, the one who was seasonal taught you that seasons change but God remains the same, and the one who was exclusive taught you the power and love that are given through a simple invite. Instead of becoming bitter, become better from the friendship ending.

Hebrews 13:8 says, "Jesus Christ is the same yesterday and today and forever." Some friendships may end, but Jesus Christ will always remain the same. Be thankful that God used that friend at that time to make you better and that your Savior won't ever change.

You don't need to force a friendship
that no longer fits.

the better friend challenge

- When have you experienced a friendship breakup? How did it make you feel?

- How is it challenging for you to trust that God is doing something new in your life?

- Paul and Barnabas had a disagreement that led to a split, and both ended up going where God wanted them. How might your friendship breakups lead you and your former friend to where you're supposed to be?

- What does it look like to have a pure and hopeful heart after friendship breakups?

truth 10

sometimes we're the bad friend

At one point or another, we've all been the bad friend.

"Who's coming tonight? Are Caroline, Lauren, and Ansley coming too?" I asked.

My friends looked at me, annoyed. "Grace, for the hundredth time, her name is pronounced *Ain*sley."

Ainsley was in a smaller group of friends from my college sorority. She was kind, inviting, funny, and sweet, yet I had one problem: I always mispronounced her name. I will say, I was the child who was in speech therapy until the seventh grade. I also was tongue-tied till eighth grade—my tongue was literally attached to the bottom of my mouth, and I had to get it lasered. Words haven't always been easy for me to pronounce, but if I'm being honest, when I mispronounced Ainsley's name, it was because of laziness. And everyone saw my lack of care.

After we graduated, we were all invited to a wedding. Another friend reminded me, "Grace, do not forget her name is pronounced *Ain*sley."

"What do you mean? I've been saying it that way."

Everyone jumped into the conversation then and reminded me I didn't usually pronounce it right. Not only was I not kind enough to work on pronouncing her name, but I also wasn't sensitive enough to realize I had been hurting her feelings repeatedly by not working on this.

I showed up to the wedding way more mature. Having rehearsed her name about fifty-four times prior, I gave her a big hug and said, "Ainsley, I missed you!"

She smiled and could tell I had practiced her name. And just like that, I had recognized my flaw, fixed it, and approached my friend kindly.

Later, when she came to Dallas with some friends to support me at my book event, we actually discussed my years of pronouncing her name wrong. She was kind about it, but she confirmed my earlier realization that what had hurt her wasn't my inability to pronounce her name but my choice for years to not care and fix it.

There's a story in the Bible about God talking to a woman named Hagar who had been overlooked, hurt, and cast aside. She was running away from an abusive situation, and at her lowest moment, God called her by name. The Creator of the universe spoke her name. And in return, she called God "the God who sees me."[1]

God calls us all by name, and He sees us. He is "the God who sees me," and He sees Ainsley. He knows how to pronounce her name. It was rude and lazy of me to not try.

I've been the bad friend in more ways than forgetting how to pronounce someone's name. I've hurt my friends' feelings, said the wrong things, and had to apologize for my actions. It is sometimes hard for us to remember that we have been the bad friend too. And it is hard for us to give grace to our friends if we don't remember the grace we have received from both God and the people who know us.

It is hard for us to give grace to our friends if we don't remember the grace we have received from both God and the people who know us.

To see and know others is one of the most important actions we can continually take in friendships. We model our friendships after Jesus, the one who sees and knows us. However, because we are human, we will fail our friends. We will slip up in big and small ways. When we fail to see and know someone, we selfishly choose laziness over care.

You will inevitably be a bad friend. There is no doubt about it. But it is important in those moments to seek reconciliation, ask for grace, and work on using the lesson to make you kinder and wiser in the future. Let mistakes help you know your friend better. Let your need to ask for grace remind you of the grace God gives you daily as well as the grace you need to give your friends when they slip up.

The Enemy wants to keep us stuck in shame or ignorance. Shame tells us that there is no hope in trying to be better and no grace that can forgive us. Ignorance tells us that we are above the need for grace and growth.

I once lied to a friend. I was struggling with finances, and in my stress, I went behind her back and tried to get her current roommate and close friend to live with me. Of course, this came across to my friend as selfish and unkind. At first, I felt shame because, to be honest, I knew I was being sneaky. Part of me wanted to forget the whole thing, avoid the hard conversation I knew I should have, and move on as soon as possible without trying to heal the friendship. But after prayer, God transformed my shame into conviction, and I realized what I needed to do to seek reconciliation:

- pray before the conversation
- humbly admit where I went wrong and be bold enough to share why
- ask for forgiveness and respect my friend if she wanted time and space to process
- share my heart for moving forward

With this friend I lied to, I prayed before the conversation and felt compelled to be honest and tell her I was between jobs and struggling financially. I asked for forgiveness and explained that I understood if she didn't trust me but that I wanted to move forward and be better. This friend realized I went behind her back not because I was mad or trying to trick her but because I was in a hard place. She empathized and gave me grace. Was it vulnerable to admit what I was going through? Oh yes. But it was holy and good, and our friendship moved forward.

Matthew 18:15–17 says, "If your brother or sister sins, go and point out their fault, just between the two of you. If they listen to you, you have won them over. But if they will not listen, take one or two others along, so that 'every matter may be established by the testimony of two or three witnesses.' If they still refuse to listen, tell it to the church; and if they refuse to listen even to the church, treat them as you would a pagan or a tax collector."

Be thankful for friends who point out your sin privately and are brave enough to share their hurt privately with you as well.

If you need to involve a third party, that can be beneficial to bring wisdom into a hard conversation. Remember, hard doesn't mean bad. Hard conversations can be holy and make friendship stronger.

Give unreasonable grace to those God has purposefully placed in your life, and praise God for friends who give grace to you.

We should always try to wake up and become kinder, better, and more purposeful people and friends and to live in a way that sees and knows both our God and the people around us. Every day is a new opportunity to learn, grow in wisdom, and become better, but only if you allow both God and His people to help you become better. God calls you by name and seeks to know your restless heart, so seek to know and see your friends well. When you mess up, ask for grace, and remember the beautiful truth that grace isn't fair. Give unreasonable grace to those God has purposefully placed in your life, and praise God for friends who give grace to you.

7 ways
to handle reconciliation

When I was about eight years old, I got into a kid fight with my neighbor and best friend at the time. I can't remember what it was about. I am sure I was overly sensitive, but I remember her calling me on my home phone and apologizing. Five minutes after the fight, we were back to riding in her Barbie Jeep and laughing.

During high school, I had a fight with my best friend. There was a betrayal, and we talked about the fight to everyone but each other. I think even her mom posted a Facebook status about me. One day, we decided it was easier to be "friends" than to stay mad at each other, but we never talked about our hurts and never truly reconciled. The shallow friendship only got worse, and our lack of reconciliation caused more problems later on. *Shocking, right?*

In college, my best friend Britta and I got into a fight over something I can't even remember. While driving back from a long road trip, we finally talked it out. Britta will be my matron of honor one day. Our reconciliation protected our friendship.

Too often, we stress about how to make friends so much that we forget to prepare our hearts for how to keep friends. Reconciliation is crucial for any and every friendship. Because we are broken, confusion, disagreements, and tension will probably arise. It is up to us to ask God for wisdom in times of trouble. If wisdom doesn't show up, then conflict will.

If we want better friendships, we need to have the tools to handle reconciliation before the need arises. If you forget to prepare for conflict, you might run away from it and even lose a friendship. So together, let's look at seven ways to handle reconciliation.

1. Pray before reconciliation. Prayer is crucial for your friendships. Don't just pray for the right words; pray for your friend, for God's hand over their life, and for humility in

your heart and words. Pray for both of you. When you pray for your friend to receive God's best, you are reminded that you are teammates, not competitors.

2. Set up a private conversation. Don't merely text "We need to talk." A message like that can set your friend in a defensive posture before the first words are even spoken. Ask for a meetup, and be clear that you have felt a need for a reconciliation. Clearly explain ahead of time that your goal is to reconnect and to listen to them as well.

3. Confess your sin. Confession in the beginning can lead to a humble conversation. Humility is contagious. If you start reconciliation with a humble heart, the other person will likely feel safe to confess with humility too.

4. The goal of reconciliation is not to air out *all* your thoughts about the other person but to share your heart, pain, burdens, and goals. Have self-control and wisdom in what you choose to say.

5. You will never regret listening. Listening well is loving well. Pay attention to the thoughts, feelings, and struggles that your friend shares. Have a receptive heart so you can be empathetic and find ways to move forward.

6. Reconciliation should be done first in private. If there is still confusion, misunderstanding, or hurt, invite someone to act as a mediator—preferably someone who works at a church or is a spiritual leader in your life.

7. Give it to God, and go to bed. Don't overthink the conversation afterward. Pray again, and ask God to make you wiser through this reconciliation. Pray for your friend's best, but don't ruminate on every word. Let the conversation make you better, not burdened or bitter.

Conflicts are guaranteed, but keep remembering that friendship is always worth the work. Don't give up just because it isn't easy. Reconciliation is an opportunity to understand God's grace better and to learn what God wants for your future. Sometimes reconciliation ends in a ride in a Barbie Jeep or another decade of laughs and memories. Other times, reconciliation might end in friends mutually agreeing to part ways—and though breakups are hard, they might just be the right next step. Either way, in the end, true reconciliation brings peace.

Reconciliation is an opportunity to understand God's grace better and to learn what God wants for your future.

the better friend challenge

· When have you been a bad friend before? To whom and why?

· When was a time you had to ask for forgiveness? What did it teach you about others and God?

· How can you be a friend who sees and knows your friends well?

· Are there any friends in your life you haven't reconciled with?

truth 11

receive the blessing of friendship

When I was twenty-four years old, I juggled being a nanny, working a second job at a church, writing my third book, traveling to speak at conferences and retreats, and trying to be a friend, all while learning how to be an adult in a crazy world. In the middle of this, I got news that one of my jobs had ended, suddenly stressing my finances. I texted my roommates before I drove home, saying, "Hey, guys, I got bad news about my job at the church. I don't want to talk about it. But wanted to let you both know if I am acting weird."

I rushed to my room as soon as I could and cried under my bedsheets—which probably needed to be washed, but my full schedule left no room for personal time. I was tired of my exhausting life, and I wanted to be alone in my pain.

My roommate Maile knocked on the door. I opened it to hear her say with tears, "I am so sorry this happened to you."

Maile remembered my past hurts and knew that this moment brought out my insecurities and fears. She was crying, knowing what I was going through. She gave me a hug, and suddenly I was crying more. I shared the hurt. She reminded me of God's goodness, told me this would be the best thing to happen to me, and encouraged me to trust that God had something better ahead. Maile knew me well enough to know that being alone wasn't what I needed. I needed her to show up and care for me. Her action reminded me that jobs and seasons change—but friends who love you well leave an imprint. I don't remember my last assignment for that part-time job that helped pay the bills, but I will forever remember the way Maile cared for me that Wednesday afternoon in my messy room.

There's a Bible story about a few men who went out of their way to bring a friend who couldn't walk to Jesus.[1] They heard that Jesus was passing through their town and that He was capable of healing, so they brought their friend to Him. But there was one problem: The crowd around Jesus was so thick, it was impossible to get close to Him. So instead, they carried their friend up to the roof, made an opening, and lowered him to Jesus. Jesus healed their friend from both his sins and his inability to walk. Jesus told the friends that the man had been healed because of their faith. The big crowd surrounding them was amazed and came to know the power of Jesus.

When Maile knocked on my door, despite the barrier I created and even the lie of saying I didn't want to talk about it, she brought me to Jesus. She broke through the roof—well, my locked door—and cared for my soul and my healing and brought me to His feet.

I used to hear this Bible story and envision myself being the kind of friend who brought others to Jesus. Although that has also been me, I can't forget about the times when I was the one my friends brought to Him. I was the one who received the healing and love I needed. We talk so often about how we should give grace, have boundaries, and be loving, but we also can't forget to receive the gift and blessing of friendship.

In our culture, we don't like to share our hard times with

others. We want to seem like we have it all together and like we don't need help. We want to be the superheroes in the stories. However, we weren't called to be the superheroes. We were meant to both give and receive friendship. And when you humbly accept love from your friends, you inspire others to experience the kind of rich friendship God created us for.

> *When you humbly accept love from your friends, you inspire others to experience the kind of rich friendship God created us for.*

I have become better through receiving the gift of friendship. And one of the most powerful benefits of learning to receive friendship is that we learn how to receive the friendship of God too. Maile felt what I felt and showed me her care through her emotions. Christ does this too. Hebrews 4:15–16 even says, "We do not have a high priest who is unable to empathize with our weaknesses, but we have one who has been tempted in every way, just as we are—yet he did not sin. Let us then approach God's throne of grace with confidence, so that we may receive mercy and find grace to help us in our time of need." Our Savior came to this earth, felt the worldly hurts, and can empathize with us. A posture of empathy shows care. Our perfect Savior can empathize, so we should not only empathize with our friends but also accept our friends' empathy. We can run to God's throne of grace with confidence that there is healing. We can lean on our friends to bring us to His throne.

When I went through a breakup, my friend who married young sent me a gift, wrote me a letter, and called me. She was so sad for me. I wanted to roll my eyes and tell her she didn't understand since she hadn't been single for a while. Then I realized the Enemy was trying to lie to me. Her pains had been different, but her empathy was real. Her care was real. I couldn't give the Enemy the power to separate us. Empathy doesn't mean that our friends have had the same issues, lives, or situations but that they choose to bear our burdens and weep with us.

> *Empathy doesn't mean that our friends have had the same issues, lives, or situations but that they choose to bear our burdens and weep with us.*

We've mentioned this verse already, but I think it is so powerful in friendships. Romans 12:15 says, "Rejoice with those who rejoice, weep with those who weep" (ESV). Friendships are powerful when you are okay with your differences, empathize with your friends' pains, and celebrate their joys. I have celebrated my friends who got married when that was my prayerful request to God for them. At first, I was scared it would be hard for me, but then I realized I had prayed for this to come. We should be praying so hard for our friends that we rejoice when God shows up and gives them miracles.

Remember, there is beauty in accepting the blessing of friendship. You become better when you allow your friends to make you better. Don't become so good at handling things on your own that you push away the very blessing God has for you.

> *Don't become so good at handling things on your own that you push away the very blessing God has for you.*

7 reminders
about accepting love better

"Grace, friendship isn't about you being the hero." An older mentor said this to me in a season where I wanted to be the best friend ever. I wanted others to see me and think, *Dang, Grace is a good friend and cares so much. She juggles her job and her life and still shows up every day for her people.* If there were a "most likely to pick you up on the side of the road and always care for you well" award, I wanted it. I cared so much about showing up for my friends. At one point in my life, I was annoyed when I was the better friend, feeling pathetic for trying so hard. But then it flipped in another unhealthy direction: I became obsessed with being the *best* friend. I planned multiple bachelorette parties, surprised my friends states away, and tried to remember every detail. I listened to their problems but didn't want to bother them with mine. The truth is, some of the people in my life loved this and needed this. But in this obsession, I forgot that my friends were also trying to be good friends to me. They needed to experience the joy of being the hands and feet of Jesus to someone they cared about.

At one of the parties I hosted, I was trying to prepare everything perfectly. I wanted everyone to come to my house for a girls' night and have the best time. So, I started cooking a lovely salmon dish with lemons, cilantro, and honey to go with pasta and a salad. Everyone began to show up and mingle, and I was trying to juggle all there was to do. Friends would come up to me and ask, "Grace, do you need any help?" And I would shoo them away, saying, "No, go mingle and have fun. I am almost done."

The truth was, I was not almost done. Time went by, and suddenly it was 8 P.M. Everyone had mingled for over an hour, and their stomachs were growling with hunger. Finally, after juggling the many things going on in the house, I checked on the salmon. I opened the oven—and realized I had accidentally set the oven to broil! The lemon, so beautifully placed on top of the salmon, was burnt to a crisp.

It can't be that bad, I thought.

While my hungry guests mingled some more, I placed my fork in the salmon and realized this was the driest piece of fish ever. It was bone-dry, burnt, and not good.

My friend came to check on me. "How's it going, Grace?" And I cried.

I told her about the salmon. And then in my small kitchen, I bumped the nice Volcano candle I had lit to take away the fish smell, and it cracked. *Ugh.* Now I was really crying.

Before I could speak, my friend grabbed her phone, called an Italian restaurant, ordered pasta, and left to pick it up. I tried to not ask her for help, and she didn't insist—she just did.

I cleaned myself up, wiped my tears, and mingled with everyone. We ended up eating delicious pasta and sharing laughs, and then all my friends helped me clean up. I tried to shoo them away, but the friend who had helped me in my salmon crisis looked at me sternly to remind me to accept help.

You and I were never called to be the heroes. That's God's job. Each person you meet and friend you have bear the image of God. Why don't you give them an opportunity to show you their love? No one needed me to be the perfect host; they needed me to be a loving friend. And a loving friend not only blesses her friends but also gives her friends the opportunity to bless her.

To receive the gift of friendship more, let's remember these seven truths:

1. There are reasons why it might be hard for you to receive love. Do you feel unlovable? Have you gotten used to friendships where you only give? Did your parents instill in you at a young age to depend on no one? Often we find it hard to receive either because we feel unlovable and are struggling to see our worth or because we have too much pride and think receiving help and love is showing weakness. Identify whether you're struggling with insecurity or pride.

2. You're being a blessing to your friends by allowing your friends to be a blessing to you. When I took my mentor Ms. Stacy to get her nails done while I was back in my hometown, she tried to shoo away my money. Ms. Stacy has mentored me since sixth grade, so she has bought me plenty of dinners and lunches and spent gas money to see me. So honestly, it was fulfilling for me to bless her in a small way. In response to her trying to keep me from paying, I said, "Will you let me be a blessing?" She knew she couldn't say no to that. Blessing her blessed me. Give your friends, family, and peers the opportunity to bless you. It is actually even rude of you to never let your friends be a blessing. If a friend tried to give you a gift and you refused it, she would probably be offended. Accept the blessing of friendship.

3. A perfect you will never show people your perfect Savior. In 2 Corinthians 12:9, the Bible says, "He said to me, 'My grace

is sufficient for you, for my power is made perfect in weakness.' Therefore I will boast all the more gladly about my weaknesses, so that Christ's power may rest on me." When you burn the salmon, leave your house untidy, cry over a trial you're facing, or show your humanness and vulnerability in any way, you're also showing Christ's strength. A fake you lies to people, but the real you shows others your perfect Savior.

4. Friendship is made in both giving and receiving. You will miss out on true friendship if you focus only on giving. If you don't accept help, kindness, and blessings from those who love you, you will never be known. When our friends know us, see us at our worst, recognize our weaknesses and still love us—we begin to understand Christ's love a little better.

5. Finding Christian friends who bless us shows us glimpses of heaven and the eternal love we will one day feel. Obviously, heaven will be better and the purest form of peace, but a girls' night encouraging each other, a FaceTime with a long-distance best friend, or a random check-in can help us see a glimpse of women of purity praising God together. So don't let these moments make you feel like a burden; let them feel like a reflection of eternity with God and His children. Practice allowing these moments to open your heart to God's goodness, both here and waiting for us in heaven.

6. A friend who cares enough to make you better is a gift sent from God. Cherish that friendship well. Protect it.

There are plenty of friends who will get brunch, share jokes, and maybe even plan trips with you. But it is rare to find someone who gets better with you. Celebrate the beautiful gift from God when another believer runs alongside you and grows with you. Because you are growing together, there will be confusion, hiccups, and lessons— and there will always be a need to push each other to Christ. When your friends are the blessing in your life, remember this is a gift from God above.

7. Our holy friendships make God smile. I want Him to look at my friendships with pleasure, happy that He gave His people the special gift of one another. I want Him to smile when He sees the friend who made me a friendship bracelet to celebrate a big career milestone, knowing that He used Mckenzie to show me He is proud of me. I want Him to see me accept Ms. Stacy's mentorship and to be proud that I embraced a friendship that makes me wiser and better. And I want Him to see the vulnerable phone calls with my friend Nora and beam with joy knowing that nothing can separate us from becoming better, even miles and states apart. When God's people live together in His presence, they not only become better but also reflect His love. Psalm 133:1 says, "How good and pleasant it is when God's people live together in unity!" Your unity is good, makes you better, and makes God smile, knowing that He gave you and me the gift of each other and that we recognize this gift in our day-to-day.

What is funny is that my dinner-party disaster became a moment where I saw a friend care for me. If we don't receive love from God-given friendships, we don't receive the image of Christ. So often, we ask God to speak to us, but we forget to receive His signs and His voice that come in the form of our friends. Accept the image of Christ that comes through a friend stepping in to help with dishes, wipe your tears, and listen to you talk about the same situation a million times—a friend who shows up. Don't always try to be the hero; instead, celebrate that together you and your friends are sitting at the table Jesus has prepared for you in front of your insecurity, doubt, enemies, and the chaos of a crazy week.

The same friend who helped me during that anxious moment while hosting actually bought me a candle and left it on my doorstep. I saw it the next day and laughed. It was more joyful to have her love in my life than to try to run a dinner party alone. Maybe that is also the gift of friendship: to be in relationship with people who gather our broken pieces, see us in our weakness, and make us new by loving us and pointing us to our perfect Savior.

the better friend challenge

- Is it hard for you to accept help from others? Why?

- When was a time a friend empathized with your pain? How did it make you feel?

- Do you ever struggle to believe your friends can empathize with you, because their lives look different from yours?

- What opportunities do you have right now to rejoice with friends who are rejoicing and weep with friends who are weeping?

truth 12

leave people better

My grandma lives in a small town in Florida called Madison, where there isn't much except a few stoplights, a really good Mexican restaurant, and a cute boutique called Daisy and Dukes connected to a café and owned by a local mom. My grandma has lived there for more than sixty years. I'm from south Louisiana, and when Hurricane Katrina came and destroyed many parts of my city, my family had to temporarily live with my grandma after evacuation. I attended school in Madison while we were displaced, so I, too, still have friends in this small town.

Madison is very much a drive-through city. If you pass through Madison on the way to Disney World, you probably see the exit signs for food options and think, *No way are we stopping there; they have nothing.* But they don't have nothing. They have my grandmother's best friends: Judy across the street, Bunny who bakes great chocolate chip cookies and had the best pool when I was growing up, Jenny who leads her Bible studies, and the other neighbor who drives my grandmother to get groceries. For a while, Madison was blessed enough to have my grandmother's friend Vicki, who I'd like to think was also my friend. Vicki was the kind of woman who walked around the small downtown and knew everyone. She encouraged everybody, including their children and grandchildren, and anytime we were together, she was the one to remind us to get a picture for Facebook. If I ever posted a new profile picture, even states away Vicki would hype me up and make me feel like I was Miss Universe.

Some would probably choose to live in a town bigger than Madison. I mean, there's no Chick-fil-A, and I do prefer towns that have the big HomeGoods stores I can shop in. However, my grandmother loves Madison because it has many friends and residents like Vicki. Vicki sadly passed away a couple of years ago, but she left everyone and the town better. I can still hear her talking about her granddaughter Kelly, and I still remember her big jewelry and big personality. I am better for knowing Vicki.

If you're anything like me, you probably have said, "I want to see the world." I can't help but dream about what else is out there, what views I haven't seen, and what I've missed out on, and I so desperately want to bolt into new experiences. I've lived in more than four different states. My grandmother has somehow lived in the same small city, Madison, for sixty years. However, maybe women like her and Vicki are more focused on loving their neighbors and changing the world than they are about seeing the world. Maybe to be loved and to love well is to truly see the world the way God intended.

I think the older generations got friendship right. In fact, Pew Research Center found that 49 percent of seniors aged sixty-five and older have five or more close friends and they are more satisfied than younger generations in their friendships[1]— even without phones, an obsession with social media, and kickball leagues. Maybe the key to being friends with someone isn't going on a lavish girls' trip or pretending to have it all together. Maybe as we grow older, we realize it is simply about love, humility, and becoming better together. Maybe it is because older generations live like my grandmother and Vicki. If my grandmother runs out of butter for a recipe, her first instinct isn't to go to the grocery store; it is to go to Judy's house across the street. When Vicki would run into a friend at the only women's boutique in her small town, she would get excited like it was a one-in-a-million chance. She savored the unexpected hellos with genuine conversations instead of brushing off these interactions with quick, meaningless small talk. When my grandmother found out she could no longer drive due to losing her eyesight, she humbly began leaning on her community to take her to the grocery store, to go to the bigger city for a fun Saturday, and to get out of her house. She didn't just order Ubers; she humbly had her friends care for her and make her life better.

We as friends need to be ready to love, be ready to receive, and in return leave people better. We can't be worried about being needy; we need to be in unity and community. We must find joy in random encounters, in the friends who lift us up in our time of need, and in loving the world well.

We as friends need to be ready to love, be ready to receive, and in return leave people better.

Love holds "no record of wrongs"[2] according to Scripture. When Vicki passed away, I went through the many Facebook messages we exchanged while I was far away from Madison. She would always check in on me, and I would catch up with her. However, when I look back at our messages, I see there were many times where I took a while to respond or didn't respond at all. It was not intentional; I was busy. Yet Vicki never kept a scoreboard of all the times she reached out and I didn't. She just loved well.

We get one life and one opportunity in this broken world to make a difference. You can leave this world better and loved, or you can try to "be even" with everyone else. Vicki sought a loving life, not to be even with others.

You may not live in a small town that reflects a Hallmark movie where everyone knows everyone, and you may not have a Vicki in your life who makes you and others feel seen. But even in an apartment complex, in your neighborhood, in your suburban town, or in your shiny city where no one talks to strangers, find ways to be radically loving. Find ways to be the Vicki, to hold no record of wrongs, and to make people better.

I hope and pray that in this book you found tools and advice to help you find better friendships. I pray you become a better friend, willing to show up for your friends even when it is inconvenient. I pray you receive your friends' love graciously and better than before. I pray you leave friendship breakups and hurts better. I pray you hold no record of wrongs and love better. But most importantly, when I think about you and me, I pray we leave others better. I pray our presence shows Christ's joy and loyalty. When others encounter us, I hope they feel a warmth in our friendship that reflects Christ's unconditional love.

We leave people better when we do all of this:

- show unreasonable love
- show consistent care

- live in humility that seeks to apologize and consider how we can become better
- are always slow to speak and quick to listen
- spark joy in conversations
- find a connection with everyone
- allow Christ to sanctify us daily, making us better through His power, healing, and love

Sanctified is a big word, and I'll be honest: I am in seminary classes, and for a while I kind of just pretended to understand what it meant. "Fake it till you make it," or make a D on a paper, I guess. But one day I had a friend ask me what it meant, and I knew the jig was up. I had no clue how to explain sanctification. So, after that, I researched and even asked my seminary professors what it meant. Sanctification isn't some fancy word we use to sound smart; it is a holy process that happens after we encounter grace, and it continues as we walk with Christ. Sanctification is the process where we become clean and holy and change our actions because Christ is making us more like Him. Our thoughts become more like Christ's, and our hearts and actions reflect His. Each day we walk with Christ, pray to Him, and invite Him into our lives, we become more sanctified.

A heart seeking sanctification is one walking in a holy and loving manner. This love is unreasonable, allowing us to love radically yet trust wisely. It gives us discernment and patience. It helps us become better and helps us make others better. It is holy and humble and holds no record of wrongs.

So maybe we should look to the older generation and even befriend them. A holy and humble life leads you to vibrant friendships. And these friendships help you reach your true purpose: to leave others better and to become sanctified by Christ.

I hope as you finish this book you see that God is already in the future you're stressed about.

7 truths
about healthy friendships

I wonder where you are as you finish this book. Maybe you're in your small town or in some loud apartment with upstairs neighbors who like to stomp. Maybe you're like me and near a big city but also near the suburbs and miles away from home, with some new friendships. Maybe you're in the same city you've lived in since your sophomore-year homecoming. But wherever you are, you have a deep desire for belonging.

This world isn't easy, and it is even harder to go through this world alone. You and I both know that because we have probably gone through some trials alone due to our pride or a lack of close friends. Your desire to belong is a holy one. You desire friendships that are loyal, fun, true, and genuine—this is a good thing. You probably read this book because you wanted better friendships.

I hope as you finish this book you see that God is already in the future you're stressed about. He's preparing future friendships for you, long-distance phone calls with a lifelong friend, and celebrations to come. He is leading you to people who will be with you as you grieve and maybe send Crumbl cookies to you when you go through an unexpected rejection. Healthy friendships are coming and are here if you choose to trust God's hand over your life.

This guide may be coming to an end, but the good is just beginning. With prayer, boldness, and discernment, you can and will find friendships that make you better. So, before we go, I want to remind you of seven things about healthy friendships:

1. Healthy friendships are more than possible. Even if you've only experienced toxic friendships so far, have hope that God is leading you to better. Don't let your past hurts stop you from walking in hope for your future friendships.

2. Healthy friends are teammates, not competitors. They cheer each other on, celebrate each other's wins, and weep together when one experiences a trial. Healthy friendships are certainly not perfect, and there is always grace to be given as well as love and admiration to be shared. This type of vibrant relationship helps us grow, sharpens us, and pushes us to become the best versions of ourselves.

3. Healthy friends fiercely pray for each other. When one receives a blessing, there is no jealousy, because the friend sees that God answered her prayer too. Healthy friends bring each other to the feet of Jesus.

4. Healthy friends share laughter. They share joy and adventures, and they don't need to leave their small cities to experience fun. Healthy friendships make both you and God smile. God loves to see His people in unity. Unity is a blessing and joy.

5. Healthy friendships avoid gossip and seek purity. Purity is a posture of the heart. When your hearts and your friend-

ship are pure and the foundation isn't gossip, you both will see the Lord. Matthew 5:8 says, "Blessed are the pure in heart, for they will see God." Healthy friends push each other to see the Lord, not hear the gossip.

6. Healthy friends live on mission with you. You encourage each other to be better and to live loving lives that care for the overlooked. Healthy friendships share a purpose.

7. Healthy friends are those you trust to speak kindly and honestly about you in rooms you are not in. You trust wisely and use discernment to know that your friend's intention and heart for you are a reflection of God's love.

the better friend challenge

- When did someone show you radical love? What did they do, and why did it stand out to you?

- When have you shown your love in a way that felt radical, unique, vulnerable, and brave?

- Let yourself dream about what kind of friend your future self will be. How does radical love fit into that picture, and how can you begin living out that picture today?

bonus: 7 reminders
about avoiding gossip

Throughout this book, I've referenced the damage gossip can have on a friendship. Gossip can negatively affect all friendships—whether between young girls or middle-aged women, new connections or old relationships. It's a virus. And so, for you reader friends, I want to include a bonus list about this specific topic.

A girl I met shortly after moving to Atlanta ran in the same friend group I connected with. I had heard she gossiped about me, and it honestly made me upset. Also, this girl seemed to be the type who lied about some things—actually about *a lot* of things. Have you ever met someone like that who basically lied about everything? The friendship becomes an itch you can't scratch. You want to call them out, to catch them in one of their many untruths, but group dynamics don't allow this to happen. So you avoid the issue until it comes out in the open, usually with gossip as an unwelcome companion.

This friend would lie about her career, wealth, and even church. She said she directed movies and wrote songs that went to the Grammys, while also having a thriving business career. She said she went on *American Idol* but left early by her own choice, and she told some hard-to-believe stories about crazy life hurdles. A little online searching made it easy to see her claims weren't true.

Her lies didn't make sense and definitely didn't add up. But instead of doing the right thing and distancing myself from her, I just tried to avoid the issue . . . until I talked about her. I gossiped, made assumptions, and wasn't kind. Was she telling the truth? No. But my gossip caused destruction of its own kind. Someone asked if I knew her, and I shared my real thoughts, but my real thoughts were sinful and did not need to be shared. People found out I talked about her, and of course, word got back to her. Eventually, she asked me about it, and I told her everything I said behind her back. I felt uncomfortable, but that's what I got for sinning.

In a world where so much focus is on being right, we forget that being right isn't a fruit of the Spirit. Jesus never asked you to prove that you're right. Galatians 5:22–23 says, "The fruit of the Spirit is love, joy, peace, forbearance, kindness, goodness, faithfulness, gentleness and self-control. Against such things there is no law."

If we root our friendships and conversations in gossip, we may show we are right and bring laughter, wittiness, and power to the table, but we don't bring the Holy Spirit. When I was talking about this girl, I may have shown that she was a liar, but I wasn't loving, kind, gentle, or self-controlled.

If you're like me and love reality shows where people fight and you tune in when small-town gossip at the hair salon gets juicy but have also been the target of hurtful rumors, then you, too, know how hurtful gossip can be. Gossip seems enticing at first glance; we feel in the know and included in something important. And by contrast, stepping away from such talk can make us feel like we missed out on something. But if we want better friendships, we need to rid ourselves of gossip. Below are seven reminders to help us do so. It is better to be in the Spirit than in the know. Sure, you may miss out on what mistake your ex–best friend made, and you may never know why that couple you barely even know got divorced. But wouldn't you rather be living a life in the Holy Spirit than staying caught up with all the latest? When we root ourselves in the Spirit, we show love, joy, peace, kindness, *and self-control.* The Spirit leads us to life. Gossip always leads us to destruction.

1. Ephesians 4:29 says, "Do not let any unwholesome talk come out of your mouths, but only what is helpful for building others up according to their needs, that it may benefit those who listen." If you want to be better friends, encourage each other. Don't waste your breath belittling others together. Notice that this verse says "according to their needs." You should be so engaged with your friends, your peers, your neighbors, and others you encounter that you are aware of their needs. You know what people don't need? Someone to talk about them behind their backs. That doesn't make anyone better.

2. A popular adage says, "Great minds discuss ideas, average minds discuss events, small minds discuss people." If you're wasting your breath discussing people together, you're probably not impacting anyone. Strong minds discuss not only ideas but also faith, dreams, goals, and bettering themselves. If other people are all you think and talk about, you're going to have no room for ideas, your faith, and your future. Choose to grow as a human, not waste your God-given brain focusing on shallow and potentially untrue gossip.

3. If you're constantly having the itch to gossip about a particular friend in your life, maybe you aren't meant to be

friends. If they bug you so much that it leads you to choose sin, out of respect for them and yourself it may be better to end the friendship. Your sin is your responsibility, but if distrust and annoyance consistently cause you to not be your best self, then pray for conviction, work on loving well and not proving that you're right, but in kindness walk away. Fake friendships are common because we think it is nicer to gossip about someone and pretend to be friends than to be honest and kind. Yet it is kinder to walk away from a friendship than to talk about someone behind their back. Proverbs 10:18 says, "Whoever conceals hatred with lying lips and spreads slander is a fool." I should've walked away from that friend I was gossiping about. I didn't need to transform my annoyance into sin and become a worse version of myself.

4. There's a difference between talking about something that happened to you and talking negatively about someone and gossiping. You're allowed to tell a close friend about the sins of others who have hurt you. You're allowed to confess negative feelings to friends or vent about the hurt someone else caused you. We as friends should encourage one another to be honest about what happened, share our hurt, and process the situations that overwhelm us in healthy community—but we can't indulge sin. Encourage your friend to be honest, weep with her, sit with her in her hurt and pain, but point her to how she can be better.

5. Some people will think you're less fun when you refuse to gossip. That's okay. True joy comes from knowing Jesus,

living for Him, and loving others well. Don't waste time proving you're fun; instead, seek eternal joy.

6. Chances are, if a person is willing to talk about their other friends easily, they also talk about you. I know that sounds dramatic, and I don't think making assumptions is healthy. But it is healthy to be wise. Don't be delusional and naïve and think you're different or super special; instead, use discernment. When in doubt, pray for wisdom.

7. When you speak destruction in others' lives, you'll destroy your own. If you obsess over drama, it will follow you. That sounds obvious, but I had to learn this the hard way. Every time I talked about someone and obsessed over gossip, I hurt someone, and oftentimes, I hurt myself and led myself away from peace. Gossip added anxiety to my life and caused rooms that could've been full of joy to be full of confusion and drama.

Gossip has existed since the beginning of sin. The Bible talks about gossip, hurt, and betrayal over and over again. It is like God knew that thousands of years later, there would be two girls like you and me at a mediocre Mexican restaurant, eating queso and drinking margaritas, itching to gossip about hometown drama. In this broken world, gossip will always exist. People are gossiping now and will be again in the next day, year, and decade. Gossip will always be active in this world, but it doesn't have to be active in your life. You may mess up occasionally, but if you and your friends make gossip the foundation of your friendship, then your friendship will be a picture of the broken world and not heaven.

You have the power to cultivate relationships that are small pictures of heaven and of God's gracious presence. This can only happen if you invite God into your friendships. Jesus said, "Where two or three gather in my name, there am I with them."[1] Gather in God's name together, not in the name of other people's hurts.

When you speak destruction in others' lives, you'll destroy your own.

notes

truth 1: know the difference between miserable comforters and unreasonable love

1. Stephen Chbosky, *The Perks of Being a Wallflower* (New York: MTV Books/Pocket Books, 1999), 24.
2. Job 1:1, 8; 2:3.
3. Job 16:2.
4. Job 42:7.
5. John 13:13.
6. Isaiah 9:6.

truth 2: community is created, not found

1. Aristotle, *The Nicomachean Ethics of Aristotle,* trans. J. E. C. Welldon (New York: Macmillan, 1902), 8.3–5.
2. Proverbs 17:17.
3. Galatians 5:22–23, NLT.
4. Aristotle, *The Nicomachean Ethics of Aristotle.*

truth 3: give grace, not excuses

1. Steve Siegle, "The Art of Kindness," Mayo Clinic Health System, August 17, 2023, www.mayoclinichealthsystem.org/hometown-health/speaking-of-health/the-art-of-kindness.

truth 5: don't beg to sit at tables Jesus hasn't prepared for you

1. Matthew 21:13.
2. Matthew 21:15.
3. Taylor Swift, "Cardigan," by Aaron Brooking Dessner and Taylor Swift, track 2 on *Folklore,* Republic Records, 2020.
4. John 13:35.

truth 7: **know the difference between loyal to a fault and loyal to your calling**

1.   Ruth 1:16–17, ESV.

truth 9: **friendship breakups are hard but can still be holy**

1.   John 13:1–30.

truth 10: **sometimes we're the bad friend**

1.   Genesis 16:13.

truth 11: **receive the blessing of friendship**

1.   Mark 2:3–12.

truth 12: **leave people better**

1.   Isabel Goddard, "What Does Friendship Look Like in America?," Pew Research Center, October 12, 2023, www.pewresearch.org/short-reads/2023/10/12/what-does-friendship-look-like-in-america.
2.   1 Corinthians 13:5.

bonus: **7 reminders about avoiding gossip**

1.   Matthew 18:20.

GRACE VALENTINE is a TEDx speaker and the host of the *Water into Wine* podcast, and the author of five books, including *Am I Enough?* She's a contributing writer for Proverbs 31 Ministries and Live Original. Grace grew up near New Orleans, Louisiana, and graduated from Baylor University with a degree in journalism. She now lives in Atlanta, Georgia, and is earning a degree at Asbury Theological Seminary. Her mission is to show others that Christianity is an adventure worth living.